The Summer Camp SURVIVAL GUIDE

Cool Games, Camp Classics, and How to Capture the Flag

BY
Chris Pallatto
AND
Ron DeFazio

ILLUSTRATED BY
Ethan Long

The
Summer Camp
SURVIVAL GUIDE

Cool Games, Camp Classics, and How to Capture the Flag

BY **Chris Pallatto**

AND

Ron DeFazio

ILLUSTRATED BY

Ethan Long

STERLING

New York / London
www.sterlingpublishing.com/kids

For Alana, Skylar, Jaxson, and all those people whose life soundtracks
include at least one neato-repeato.—R.D.

Thanks to "Sloper John" Myers for inspiring my professional camp career and
the crew at YMCA Camp Mataucha for bringing out the best in me.
This book is for Kelly, Cayden, and Gavin.—C.P.

For Kevin and Natalie.—E.L.

STERLING and the distinctive Sterling logo are registered trademarks of
Sterling Publishing Co., Inc.

Library of Congress Cataloging-in-Publication Data
Pallatto, Chris.
The summer camp survival guide / Chris Pallatto and Ron DeFazio ; illustrated by Ethan Long.
p. cm.
Includes index.
ISBN 978-1-4027-4912-4
1. Camps--Juvenile literature. I. DeFazio, Ron. II. Long, Ethan, ill. III. Title.
GV192.2.P35 2009   796.54--dc22   2008008865

Lot #:
2   4   6   8   10   9   7   5   3   1
02/10
Published by Sterling Publishing Co., Inc.
387 Park Avenue South, New York, NY 10016
Text © 2010 by Chris Pallatto and Ron DeFazio
Illustrations © 2010 by Ethan Long
Distributed in Canada by Sterling Publishing
c/o Canadian Manda Group, 165 Dufferin Street
Toronto, Ontario, Canada M6K 3H6
Distributed in the United Kingdom by GMC Distribution Services
Castle Place, 166 High Street, Lewes, East Sussex, England BN7 1XU
Distributed in Australia by Capricorn Link (Australia) Pty. Ltd.
P.O. Box 704, Windsor, NSW 2756, Australia

Sterling ISBN 978-1-4027-4912-4

For information about custom editions, special sales, premium and
corporate purchases, please contact Sterling Special Sales
Department at 800-805-5489 or specialsales@sterlingpublishing.com.

CONTENTS

A Note from Peter Surgenor
President, American Camp Association

winkling stars and campfire songs. Taking a hike and looking for birds and trees. Splashing in a lake and finding out your new friend loves the same things you do. These are experiences from camp—ones that many people share and ones that are intensely personal—that children never forget.

When children play, they also learn. First-hand experience is unmatched as a teacher. The camp community knows this, as we have been providing children with opportunities to learn through play for nearly 150 years. Creative play is healthy and essential. With more and more time spent sitting in front of a screen—whether at a TV or a computer—and a sometimes heavy dose of scheduled activities, kids are missing out on free and unstructured play. This kind of experience is critical if children are to reach important developmental milestones. When children play, they learn by actively doing— they explore and discover, learn to get along with others, take safe risks, try new things and maybe fail, but learn to try again.

Camp allows children to build skills necessary to prepare them to assume roles as successful adults. The American Camp Association's (ACA's) independent research supports this—children who go to camp, even for as little as one week each summer, show growth in areas such as self-confidence, independence, making friends, exploring and learning new activities, and spirituality.

The camp experience provides a unique environment that allows kids to be kids. It's a very special place where a child's individual mental, emotional, and physical needs are nurtured. The benefits of these experiences translate not only into the classroom, but also into every aspect of a child's life—and are carried on into adulthood. Camp is an experience that truly lasts a lifetime.

The Summer Camp Survival Guide: Cool Games, Camp Classics, and How to Capture the Flag, by Chris Pallatto and Ron DeFazio, will take you through the whirlwind of summer camp—all the wacky songs, fun-filled games, and special friendships. The book gives tips from enrolling in the right camp to getting the most fun out of your summer, and also calls upon the importance of the camp experience in a child's life.

ACA works to preserve, promote, and enhance the camp experience for all children and adults. ACA-Accredited camp programs ensure that children are provided with a diversity of educational and developmentally challenging learning opportunities. These camp programs and many tips for preparing for camp can be found on ACA's family-oriented Web site, www.CampParents.org.

On behalf of ACA, we look forward to welcoming your child to a memorable camp experience—whether for the first time or a return visit!

Let the Adventure Begin!
from Ron DeFazio:

Are you the kind of kid who runs to the pool and jumps right in, or do you like to feel the water first with your toes? Would you want the lead role in a play, or would you rather build the sets? Do you like to make dozens of friends, or do you have one or two best friends who know everything about you?

Whatever type of kid you are, if you're heading off to camp, this book is for you!

The guidebook now in your hands can help you get ready for a great summer at camp. In these pages, you'll get a sneak peek at what's in store for you when you get to camp. The cool chapters and sections in this book will help you have the best summer ever. You'll find packing tips, learn how to make friends, discover songs and games, and be introduced to all kinds of people.

Keep an eye on our pal, C.D., who will offer some tips of his own. Happy camping!

Hi, I'm CD, and I'm here to show you the ins and outs of summer camp!

from Chris Pallatto:

When you're getting ready to go to summer camp, you may have two different reactions.

If you're new to camp, you might feel nervous and wonder:

"What will I do?"
"I won't have any friends!"
"It will be boring."
"I'll miss my family."

If you're returning to camp, you'll probably feel excited and think:

"I wonder what's new at camp this year?"
"I can't wait to see all of my friends!"
"I've been waiting ALL year for this!"
"I can't wait to sleep over—the nighttime is the best part."

It's perfectly normal to be nervous about going to summer camp. After all, you probably feel most comfortable staying at home and doing the same things you've done every summer. We promise that once you've experienced summer camp, you won't be able to imagine a summer without it!

Where else but summer camp can you spend the day making a pirate costume,

looking for dinosaur bones, or competing in an international burping contest? Where else can you sing songs, build forts, and roast marshmallows all in the same day? Nowhere, of course!

Summer camp is a fun experience, filled with exciting adventures, goofy traditions, and great friends. It's the place for playing exciting games, singing silly songs, and just simply having fun. For new campers, this book is part "sneak peak" and part "survival guide." You'll learn about the games, songs, and traditions you'll experience at summer camp, as well as ways to prepare for the summer, make friends, stay in touch with your family, and more.

By the end of this book, you'll know what bug juice is, why camp directors always carry around a clipboard, and the words to "Magdalena Hagdelena." By the end of the summer, you'll wonder how you are going to stand the wait until next year. Let the adventure begin!

CHAPTER 1

MAKING THE BIG DECISION

So you think you want to go to summer camp?

The Nitty-Gritty about Choosing a Summer Camp

S ummer camp can be a great experience for both camper and parents. It can be one filled with adventures, new friends, and endless activities. There are many camp choices available, ranging from sports camps to resident camps. The goal is to find a camp that best matches your needs and interests.

There is an appropriate camp for a camper of any age—some kids start going to camp as early as 5 years old. Choosing the correct camp is dependent on the camper's comfort level, the activities planned at a particular type of camp, and the camp's ability to provide a safe and rewarding experience.

We recommend that you choose a camp that has been accredited by the American Camp Association (ACA) or a similar organization in your country, such as the Canadian Camp Association or Ontario Camping Association. Please see the "Questions to Ask Camp Directors" section for more information about this important process.

Are You Ready for the Adventure?

Campers of any age may be nervous about going to camp, but that doesn't necessarily mean that the time isn't right. Traditional summer camps focus primarily on building friendships and providing fun activities. First-time campers should ask themselves the following questions to determine if they are ready for camp:

* Do I enjoy meeting new people at school or in my community?

* Do I look forward to going to activities that may have other kids present, such as family parties or company picnics?

* Do I make friends easily?

If you answered "yes" to any of the questions, it is likely that you are ready to give camp a try.

Pre-camp jitters are normal. And children who are typically social or comfortable around other children will generally be successful in a camp setting.

If you answered "no" to most of the questions, consider the following tips:

* Try to choose a camp with a friend from school or the neighborhood. If you are nervous in new situations, it will really help to have a friend to experience them with.

* Choose the camp that most closely matches your interests (see the "Choosing the Best Summer Camp for Your Child" section). Although Dad or Mom's first choice may be his or her own childhood camp, you may want to sign up for one that meets your own needs. Try a local one that specializes in something that interests you, like a basketball or computer camp.

* Choose a camp that is shortest in duration. Many camps offer trial weeks or half-day programs. For first-timers, this may be a good option.

* It's important that both adults and future campers alike are involved in the camp selection process, including open houses, reviewing literature, and meeting the staff.

A word about camp movies...

Camp movies are great fun to watch, and make camp seem like a lot of fun. However, they often make light of all of the hard work and professionalism that real camp owners, directors, and staff demonstrate in true camp settings. Campers will most likely enjoy true-to-life adventures and make lifelong friends under the watchful eye of responsible camp staff. So, watch *Meatballs* and *Ernest Goes to Camp* with a bowl of popcorn, but rest assured that real camps meet a much higher standard.

SPECIAL TEAR-OUT SECTION FOR PARENTS!

Choosing the Best Summer Camp for Your Child

The key to a great summer camp experience is finding a match that meets your family's needs and budget and your child's interests. Be sure to include your child in the selection process to ensure a smooth transition from school to camp.

Create a list of possible camps based on the following:

* **Price and location.** Basically, the list can initially be whittled down to camps that your family can afford. Don't despair: price is not the best indicator of quality. There are plenty of great camps that operate on a shoe-string budget. Remember, you're only creating a list in this step and you'll examine quality below.

* **Activities.** Review various camp descriptions and daily schedules, and identify the ones that offer activities that most closely meet your child's interests.

* **Location and convenience.** When parents choose a day camp, they usually base their choice on how easy it will be to transport their children to the camp on a regular basis. Families often choose a resident camp that is close enough to meet their distance and travel comfort level. Many parents want their child to experience being away from home but also want them to go to camp close enough so they can visit on family day or be available in the event of an emergency.

* **Special Needs.** Many camps accommodate campers with a wide range of special needs, ranging from diet to serious medical conditions, such as cancer or diabetes. Based on your meeting with the camp staff, and the experience and focus of the camp, you may be able to find a place that suits your child.

Do a thorough camp review! Once you've created a list of summer camp options, it is important that you give each camp a thorough review. You want to know that a prospective camp is safe and rewarding.

* **Get references.** The best way to find out about a particular camp is to ask for independent feedback from others either who have sent their children to the camp, or who are knowledgeable about the camp's reputation.

  ◎ Start by checking with friends, family, and co-workers. Ask them "How did Jose enjoy Camp Mataucha?" "What types of activities did your children do?" "Were you unhappy about anything?" "What were your concerns?"

  ◎ Ask your child's pediatrician about the most popular camps with his or her patients. Children need to have a physical before they go to summer camp. Chances are your pediatrician completes lots of examinations before the summer, and hears a lot of camp stories during that time.

  ◎ Talk to the secretary at your child's school, who is also likely to hear a great deal from parents and kids about the summer camp choices available in your area.

  ◎ If you have a chance, ask a current camper about the program. Ask, "What do you like about the camp?" or "Tell me about the camp counselors."

* **Go to an Open House.**

  ◎ If possible, you want to visit the camp if they offer an open house. This is a great opportunity to see the camp, meet the staff, and ask questions.

⊙ Bring your child to the open house. This is an opportunity for everyone to get comfortable with a new camp, and get excited for the upcoming summer.

⊙ Ask questions from the American Camp Association's "Questions to Ask Camp Directors" section on the next page.

✳ **Attend Camp Fairs, In-House Visits, or Staff Phone Conferences.**

⊙ Open houses aren't possible for many resident camps. Many are located too far off the beaten path, and families simply can't make the trip. Many resident camps directors set up booths at camp fairs, and some conduct in-home visits or staff phone conferences.

⊙ Oftentimes camp directors ask returning families to coordinate in-home meetings with their friends and neighbors to discuss the camp. Generally, these families are willing to coordinate the meeting because they have a positive relationship with the camp.

⊙ If you can't attend a camp fair, or be part of an in-home visit, set up a time to discuss the camp with the director or another senior staff member.

Here are some great Web sites to check out for more information:

www.campparents.org
(American Camp Association)

www.ccamping.org
(Canadian Camping Association)

www.ontariocamps.ca
(Ontario Camping Association)

www.kidscamps.com
www.mysummercamps.com

The American Camp Association's "Questions to Ask Camp Directors"

When you receive a camp's brochure, you will invariably have questions for the camp director. From that first phone call or letter, you begin developing an impression of what a particular camp is like and how it is run. A camp may be described in nothing less than glowing terms in its brochure. The setting may be absolutely breathtaking. Activities may run the gamut from racquetball to modern dance. In the end, however, it's the human equation of how those activities are operated and conducted that determines the quality of the camp program. Get to know the camp director as a person through telephone conversations, correspondence, and a personal visit. Have the director describe the camp's philosophy and how the staff implements it.

What is the camp's philosophy and program emphasis?

Each camp has its own method of constructing programs based on its philosophy. Does it complement your own parenting philosophy? Many camps actively promote competition and healthy rivalry among camp teams, as reflected in team sports. For many campers, this is pure fun. Some parents feel that learning to be competitive at an early age teaches essential survival skills. However, other parents and educators are in favor of cooperative learning. Knowing your child's personality and style of learning is valuable in selecting the right camp.

What is the camp director's background?

ACA minimum standards recommend directors possess a bachelor's degree, have completed in-service training within the past three years, and have at least 16 weeks of camp administrative experience before assuming the responsibilities of director.

What training do counselors receive?

At a minimum, camp staff should be trained in safety regulations, emergency procedures and communication, behavior management techniques, child abuse prevention, appropriate staff and camper behavior, and specific procedures for supervision.

What is the counselor-to-camper ratio?

ACA standards require different ratios for varying ages and special needs. Generally, the ratios at resident camps are usually: one staff member for every five campers ages 4 and 5; one staff member for every six campers ages 6 to 8; one staff member for every eight campers ages 9 to 14; and one staff member for every 10 campers ages 15 to 18. At day camps the ratios are usually: one staff member for every six campers ages 4 and 5; one staff member for every eight campers ages 6 to 8; one staff member for every 10 campers ages 9 to 14; and one staff member for every 12 campers ages 15 to 18.

What are the ages of the counselors?

ACA standards recommend that 80 percent or more of the counselor/program staff be at least 18 years old. Staff must be at least 16 years old, and be at least two years older than the campers with whom they work. In Special Needs Camps, 100 percent of the counselor/program staff must be at least 18 years old.

What are desired qualities in camp staff?

The same qualities of trustworthiness and dependability sought by any employer are valued commodities in camp employees. Also, the ability to adapt to a variety of situations, empathy for and ability to work with camp clientele, a strong self-image, and an outgoing personality are important characteristics for camp staff.

What percentage of the counselors returned from last year?

Most camps have from 40 to 60 percent returning staff. If the rate is lower, find out why.

How are behavioral and disciplinary problems handled?

This is where the director's philosophy comes through loud and clear. Positive reinforcement, assertive role modeling, and a sense of fair play are generally regarded as key components of camp counseling and leadership. Rules are necessary in any organization, and the disciplinary approach taken should be reasonable and well communicated. If penalties are involved for violations, they should be applied quickly, fairly, calmly, and without undue criticism to campers.

How does the camp handle special needs?

If your child has special requirements, ask the camp director about needed provisions and facilities. Is there a nurse on staff? Do they have a designated place to store insulin or allergy medicine? Are special foods available for campers with restricted diets? Every question and each answer is important.

How does the camp handle homesickness and other adjustment issues?

Again, the camp's philosophy on helping children adjust is important. Be sure you are comfortable with the camp's guidelines on parent/child contact.

What about references?

This is generally one of the best ways to check a camp's reputation and service record. Directors should be happy to provide references.

Does the American Camp Association accredit the camp?

It is only logical that members of your family attend an ACA-Accredited® camp. Accreditation visitors ask the questions—up to 300 of them— regarding essential health, safety, and program quality issues important to a camp's overall operation. This does not guarantee a risk-free environment, but it's some of the best evidence parents have of a camp's commitment to a safe and nurturing environment for their children.

For more information on camp accreditation, please visit the ACA's Web site at www.CampParents.org or call 1-800-428-CAMP.

Reprinted from www.CampParents.org by permission of the American Camp Association; copyright 2007 American Camping Association, Inc.

Notes

CHAPTER 2

PRE-CAMP PREP

Getting Ready for the Big Adventure!

Crash Course in Summer Camps

 he chart below summarizes the most common types of summer camp choices, and the pros and cons of each.

Type of Camp	Brief Description	Pros and Cons
SLEEP AWAY CAMP (also referred to as Resident Camp)	Resident camps usually have the traditional camp activities (archery, boating, crafts, swimming, and hiking), as well as a wide range of specialty activities, such as water skiing or horseback riding. Campers who attend these camps spend one or more weeks living at camp. Campers at Resident camps come from all over the country (and the world) to attend.	**PROS** ∗ You'll really get to know the other campers of your group because you'll live with them. ∗ Resident camps tend to have more activities, simply because there is more time to do them. **CONS** ∗ You will live away from home for a period of time and won't see your family or friends until you come back. ∗ Resident camps are often more expensive than most day camps.
DAY CAMP	At day camp, campers go home at the end of each day. Day camps are usually located in towns close to your home. Traditional day camps also have the traditional camp activities (archery, boating, crafts, swimming, and hiking), as well as a wide range of specialty activities, such as water skiing or horseback riding. However, some day camps are located at schools, parks, or recreational centers and have limited activities.	**PROS** ∗ You get to go home each day, which allows you to see your friends and play on local sports teams. ∗ Day camps are usually less expensive than resident camps, which makes it easier to attend more weeks. **CONS** ∗ You may have less time for camp activities simply because you have limited time during the camp day. ∗ The fun eventually stops and you have to go home for the day and see your little sister or brother.

Type of Camp	Brief Description	Pros and Cons
TRAVEL OR ADVENTURE CAMPS	Campers spend most or all of their time away from the camp site. Campers generally meet the staff and fellow campers at the camp, and travel for the remainder of their camp experience. Travel camps take campers all over the world for a variety of fun experiences, such as rock climbing, kayaking, sightseeing, skiing, research, and more.	**PROS** ✳ You get to see and do amazing things that you can't do in your neighborhood. ✳ If you like to be independent and go on adventures, travel camp is a perfect fit. **CONS** ✳ You will be away from home for an extended period of time, ranging from several days to several weeks. ✳ Travel camps may be expensive, depending on the method of travel and the activities.
SPORTS CAMP	Sports camps are designed to give campers an opportunity to develop or improve athletic skills through lots of play and practice. Some sports camps are sport-specific, like basketball camp, soccer camp, or wrestling camp. Campers at these camps are intent on improving their athletic skills. Often, these camps are very competitive, and have highly qualified local, regional, or national coaches. Other sports camps offer campers a menu of sports to choose from weekly, such as hockey, golf, or basketball. The camper then spends the week participating in the several sports that he or she has chosen. Some sports camps take place at local colleges or high schools, and others at summer camp facilities specifically designed for sports.	**PROS** ✳ You will get your fill of sports and develop your skills! ✳ The other campers will enjoy playing sports as much as you do, so you know you'll have something in common with the other kids. **CONS** ✳ You may not be able to do many traditional summer camp activities, such as archery or boating. Many sports camps do include traditional camp activities, so be sure to ask. ✳ You may not enjoy the intensity of playing sports all day, every day.

Type of Camp	Brief Description	Pros and Cons
ARTS CAMP RESIDENT CAMP DAY CAMP	Do you want to sing or dance on stage, star in a rock band, or learn how to create beautiful pottery? If so, an arts camp might be for you. Arts camps are similar to sports camps, because they offer extensive programming in a particular field of visual or performing art, such as painting, dance, or drama. These programs are taught by experienced instructors, and you can specialize in your favorite form of art. Other arts camps let you choose several disciplines to take at the same time. For example, some camps let you take set design, vocal training, and video production if you have many different interests. Some arts camps are held at local colleges or dance studios, and others at traditional summer camps with arts programs.	**PROS** ✳ You will be able to be on stage, perform in a concert, or display your art masterpiece! ✳ You will meet other cool kids who are interested in the same hobbies as you. **CONS** ✳ You may not be able to do many traditional summer camp activities, such as archery or boating. Some specialty camps do include traditional camp activities, so be sure to ask. ✳ You may not enjoy the specific performance or projects that are selected by the camp staff. However, most camps offer interesting choices to ensure that you enjoy your activities.
ACADEMIC/ COLLEGE PREP CAMP RESIDENT CAMP DAY CAMP	Leave it to summer camps to make learning fun. These camps teach valuable skills through interesting, hands-on programs, such as crime scene investigation, Web site design, robotics, how to start a business, and more. Some programs are designed to teach you specific topics to improve your grades, pass your exams, or help you get into college. Others offer a more broad educational experience.	**PROS** ✳ You will have a great experience to put on your college resume. ✳ You will be able to impress your friends and teachers with the things you learned over the summer. **CONS** ✳ Some campers find that the ideas or topics are very challenging. Some campers enjoy being challenged with difficult projects during the summer, and others don't.
SPECIAL NEEDS CAMP RESIDENT CAMP DAY CAMP	These camps offer developmentally, physically, and medically appropriate experiences for campers with special needs, such as kids who have diabetes, cancer, or limited mobility. Typically, the camps utilize appropriately designed facilities with specialty staff to ensure that the program is both safe and fun. Many special needs camps offer the same activities offered at a traditional summer camp, modified to work with their campers.	**PROS** ✳ The activities are designed so that all campers can be included and successful. ✳ Campers will be able to make friends who have similar needs and concerns. ✳ The specially trained staff is comfortable with the medical or physical issues that a camper may have. **CONS** ✳ These camps may be expensive or hard to find.

Everything but
the Kitchen Sink

Your camp will probably provide you with a packing list of items that you will need to bring with you. Be sure to read the list carefully, because some camps require specific items or quantities based on the camp program. For example, an adventure camp may require waterproof bags for a canoe trip, while a resident camp may require that you bring all of your own bed linens.

How much is enough? Your camp will assign the quantities of different items needed. For example, some camps require that you bring enough clothes to change every day, while others have a laundry service that allows you to bring less.

Packing Secrets

Regardless of the type of camp you attend, here are two good tips:

1. **Don't bring anything valuable or breakable.** Be sure to leave your portable electronic games, cell phones, or fragile belongings at home. Camps have lots of space, dirt, and activities, and your items will be easily broken or lost.

2. **Label all of your belongings clearly.** You'll probably misplace a T-shirt or two along the way, and labels make it easy to identify them in your camp's Lost and Found pile.

Sample Resident Camp Packing List

RESIDENT CAMP

CLOTHING

shorts	socks	water shoes or sandals
long pants	underwear	
T-shirts	sneakers	rain gear and rubber boots
sweat shirts	pajamas	
hat	bathing suit	

BEDDING & LINENS

sheets	toothbrush and toothpaste	deodorant
pillow cases		nail clippers
sleeping bag	soap and shampoo	laundry bag (or use pillow case)
brush and comb	washcloth	
toiletries	towels	

Sample Resident Camp Packing List

ODDS & ENDS

flashlight

sun block

bug-repellant cream

water bottle

costumes for Theme Days

pre-stamped envelopes and stationery

sunglasses

Frisbee, etc.

For day camps, less is better. You'll have a chance to change clothes or bring items as needed every day. You have to carry everything you bring, so pack light. Besides saving your back from becoming sore, bringing only what you really need for the day helps keep you from losing your stuff!

Sample Day Camp
DAY CAMP Packing List

WEAR THESE ITEMS TO CAMP

 Hat

Sun block

Sneakers or other
closed-toe shoes

T-shirt or
long-sleeved shirt

Shorts or long pants

PACK THESE ITEMS

Bathing suit

Towel

Extra sun block

Socks

Water bottle

Lunch

Make Your Own
Packing List Here

· ·

"Countdown to Camp" Calendar

 ere are some important things to keep in mind when counting down the days 'till camp begins...

* Review camp brochure or make an appointment to visit camp.
* Make a list of activities you want to do.
* Put together pictures and favorite items that you want to bring to camp to decorate your bunk space.

* Go shopping for everything on your camp packing list.
* Label all of your belongings.
* Send your friends and grandparents a "change of address" postcard or letter with your camp address.

* Decorate your camp backpack. You can write your name on it with fancy letters or attach your favorite patches. Be sure to leave room for your camp friends to sign at the end of the summer.
* Pack your stuffed animal (so he/she doesn't miss you).
* Practice setting up your tent and rolling your sleeping bag (if you'll be camping in the woods).
* Pre-address and stamp envelopes to send to your friends and family while at camp.

* Buy a disposable camera to take pictures of all of the fun things you are going to do.

Month

Sunday	Monday	Tuesday	Wednesday	Thursday	Friday	Saturday

CHAPTER 3

GETTING SETTLED

Go Ahead, Get Comfortable!

Who's Who at Camp

amp is filled with people who have one main priority in common: to help you have a safe, fun, and exciting summer. It takes a lot of people doing a lot of different jobs to make a camp run smoothly. You might see some of these people often throughout your day, and some will be working behind the scenes. You can be sure that the people who work at your camp truly love what they are doing and are there to make your summer a memorable one.

Here Are Some of the Different Types of People You'll Meet on Your Camp Adventure:

CAMP DIRECTORS

These are the people who run your camp. **Camp directors** help out everywhere to make sure you are having a great time every day, acting as a "Mom" or "Dad" of the campgrounds. Sometimes there are one or two directors for the whole camp. They are in charge of planning all the programs and fun events at your camp and making sure that everything is running smoothly, which is why they usually carry a clipboard wherever they go. The most important job of the camp director is to make sure you're happy and comfortable, so don't be too scared to ask them for help if you need it.

COUNSELORS

Counselors are the adults who you will spend the most time with when you are at camp. They are your guides throughout your camp experience. *Your counselors* will tell you the rules of camp and help you settle in. Get to know *them* and let *them* get to know you. Remember, *your counselors* work at camp because *they* love being there and enjoy working with kids just like you. You can learn a lot from *your counselors*, and *they* are there whenever you need assistance with anything. *The counselors'* most important job, though, is to keep you safe, so stay with *them* and listen to what *they* tell you. They'll help you get off to a great start.

CAMP NURSE

Sometimes fun and games can lead to bumps and scrapes. If that happens, there is a **nurse** who can help you get back on your feet and back to the fun. Do not be afraid of the nurse, a trained professional who is there to help.

LIFEGUARDS

If you attend a camp that offers swimming, the **lifeguards** will be an important part of your camp life. Lifeguards stay by the water to keep all the campers safe while they are swimming. Sometimes the lifeguards will also be swim teachers. It's very important to listen to the lifeguards whenever you are swimming or hanging around the pool or lake.

SPECIALTY AREA DIRECTORS

Some of the most popular activities at camp are run by **specialty area directors**. These staff members are in charge of activities like rock climbing, boating and sailing, archery, arts and crafts, and the adventure/ropes course, and they're trained to give you a safe and memorable experience. These can be some of the most dangerous activities at camp, so be sure to listen to and follow all safety rules and directions. One of the best things about camp is that you will get a chance to do something that is both new and exciting. Sometimes new activities can be scary at first. Don't worry, the specialty area director will explain everything and lead you through. If after listening to all of the rules and directions you are still unsure, it is perfectly okay for you to decide not to participate. You can still cheer on all of your friends!

How to Beat Homesickness

You **didn't catch a cold, you might just be homesick.** You might be boarding the bus, or in the middle of a camp activity, and find yourself thinking about home. It might make you sad, or even upset your stomach. You may not think you'll ever feel better (we've all felt like that). But don't worry too much—homesickness eventually passes, too.

Homesickness is normal. Honestly, so many people get homesick when they are away from home: college students, professional baseball players, and, yes, campers. It's *perfectly normal* to miss your home and all of the cool friends and family who are still there! You don't have to feel silly for being homesick.

Here are a few tips to follow if you think you might get homesick:

* **Check out camp before summer starts.** We all tend to be nervous in new situations. The best way to feel at home at a new camp is to learn about the camp before you get there. This way, it won't feel so strange. Your camp probably has a Web site, brochure, and maybe even a DVD or online video for you to look at. If possible, ask your parents to bring you to an open house for a tour. You'll be able to see the camp in reality and meet some of the awesome camp staff. The more you know about the camp before you get there, the more comfortable you'll be.

* **Do something.** The best thing you can do to cure homesickness is to "take your mind off of it" by participating in camp activities. Once you start playing Capture the Flag, singing songs, or swimming, you'll find that home is the last thing on your mind. Over time, you'll be having more fun and feeling less nervous and homesick.

* **Talk about it.** Your counselor has probably seen lots of homesick campers. He or she will be able to help you feel better by listening to your concerns or giving you a new activity to concentrate on. Remember, everyone gets a little homesick—your counselor will not be surprised at all if you tell him. Sometimes talking to an adult you trust makes you feel better automatically.

* **Write home.** One of the best things to do when you miss home is to write your family a letter. Writing a letter sometimes makes you feel like you are talking with the person you are writing to. In fact, writing a letter is such a great way to cure homesickness that we've got a whole section devoted to it!

* **Hang in there!** Give camp a little time to get going. It's normal to miss your family the most when the camp session is starting. Camp can be a bit overwhelming the first day. It usually takes a few days for you to learn the routine, get to know the other campers in your group, and for camp to really get exciting. You may feel the most homesick for the first couple of days, but soon enough you and your new friends will be having tons of adventures.

Make Some New Friends

sk anyone who has been to camp and they will probably say that the best part about it is making friends. At school, you usually get only an hour each day to play with your friends at recess. However, at camp you can spend almost every moment talking, playing, or going on adventures with your friends. By the end of the summer, you'll have friends you'll remember forever.

If you are nervous about making friends at camp, here are some tips:

* **Be yourself.** The best way to make friends that you have things in common with is simply to be yourself. This means don't try to act cool, pretend to know everything, or tell lies about things you've done. Being yourself will help others trust you—which is the most important part of a good friendship. What you *can* do is show your new friends the ways in which you're unique.

* **Find other "first-timers."** When you get to camp for the first time, look for other campers who seem to be alone. Simply go up to someone who looks as lost or alone as you, say "hello," and introduce yourself. Chances are they will be relieved to have met someone, too.

* **Try new things.** At camp, you'll have an opportunity to try all kinds of activities, including lots of things you've never done before. You may be surprised at how much you'll enjoy new activities, like singing camp songs, climbing a rock wall, or playing Four-Square. Once you start participating in activities with other kids from your group, it will give you something to talk (and usually laugh) about together.

* **Follow "The Golden Rule."** Treat others how you want to be treated. Be friendly, share, be polite, and listen to others.

* **Things to avoid.** Try not to complain or be negative about activities or others. Avoid telling or listening to gossip. Do not tease or bully others, by yourself or as part of a crowd.

Break the Ice

Here are a few fun activities you can play with your new friends to get to know your fellow campers.

TWO TRUTHS AND A LIE

Have your friends try to guess which statement about yourself is false.

How to play:

1. Everyone sits in a circle.
2. Each person takes a turn telling the group three things about themselves: two that are true, and one that is a lie. Do your best to keep a straight face when you lie so that people can't tell.
3. The group discusses the statements out loud and has to agree on which one they think is the lie.
4. Once the group makes their guess, you then tell the group if they're correct. If you'd like, you can then tell them a little bit more about the true statements.
5. The game continues until everyone has had a chance.

SILENT INTERVIEWS

Tell your partner three things about yourself—without talking!

How to play:

1. Each person finds a partner within the group, and the two together move ten feet away from the other campers for some privacy.
2. Each partner takes a turn acting out three things about themselves that the other can't tell just by looking at them. For example, you can't tell your partner that you have blue eyes—that would be too easy! Try conveying to your partner that you like to go sailing, or live near the mountains, or any other fun fact about you.
3. The guessing partner then verbally guesses what he thinks the acting partner is demonstrating. The acting partner can only nod or shake his head to let the guesser know the correct or incorrect answer.
4. Once each partner has taken a turn acting and correctly guessing, they should return to the center of the group. The group should make a circle once all the partners have returned.
5. Each person then takes a turn to verbally introduce their partner to the rest of the group.

What If I Don't Like My Counselor?

t's important to understand that no matter where you go there will be people who you like more than others. Camp is no different. Remember, sometimes it takes a little while to get to know a person. Everyone deserves a chance, so try not to make a decision about someone too quickly. Take some time to get to know your counselor, just as you will with your fellow campers. You may find out that you have a lot of common interests. After all, you both like summer camp!

If you find that after getting to know your counselor, there are still things you do not like, don't be afraid to talk about it with him or her. If that doesn't work, then go talk to one of the camp directors. Your camp experience is important to them, and they will help you to make it better.

Getting Along

Just like at school or on a sports team, you might be in a group with someone you don't get along with. The best way to handle this is simply to stay away from that person as much as possible. If you can't avoid him, be polite and patient. Try to find one positive thing about the person you don't get along with, and think of that positive thing when you are with that person.

If someone is bullying you, say that you do not want to be teased or touched, and tell them to stop. If they continue, tell your counselor right away. An adult can find ways to make the situation better without embarrassing you. You're at camp to have fun, so don't let someone else ruin it for you!

CHAPTER 4

HOME SWEET CAMP

Your Home Away from Home!

Bunk Life

RESIDENT CAMP

iving at a resident summer camp is a truly unique experience. Resident camp also gives you more hours in the day to have fun, you get to know your cabin mates really well, and you get to be more grown up. Going to resident camp is a bigger responsibility than going to a day camp, too. You will have camp chores to do, more decisions to make, and less privacy than if you went home at night. You'll have to deal with snoring cabin mates, extra people with whom you need to share bathroom time, and less privacy than if you left camp at the end of the day.

However, most campers agree that the chance to be more grown up, hang out with your friends longer, and do all those extra activities are well worth the challenges of bunk life.

Cabins, Tents, and Dorms, Oh My!

The types of cabins and living quarters range from camp to camp. Some camps offer cabins that have electricity, bathrooms, fireplaces, and other fancy things. Some camps have simple cabins or platforms with tents on top and only bunks inside. Other camps use college dormitories for their living quarters, and don't have cabins at all.

Regardless of the type of living arrangements, bunk life is really about the fun you have talking, sharing, and living with your friends.

Show Your Style

Since you will be living away from home for a while, decorating your bunk or cabin can be a great way to have fun with your bunkmates, and more importantly, make you feel right at home.

1. **Put up pictures and fun items that remind you of home.** Interesting or funny items that remind you of your family and friends at home are a great way to show your new friends what you're like during the rest of the year. You can put up a family holiday card, pictures of you and your friends, postcards from favorite vacation spots, and flags from your school or favorite countries. In no time at all, your bunkmates will comment on how cool your area looks. If someone comes along to look at your wall, take the chance to share a story about home.

2. **Put up pictures and fun items that remind you of camp.** Remind yourself of why you came to camp in the first place. Pictures with your camp friends, friendship bracelets, art projects, and silly song lyrics will remind you of all the fun you're having at camp. You might have to wait until halfway through the summer to do this.

3. **Create a cabin sign.** Work with your bunkmates to create a fun welcome sign for the front of your cabin or tent. Choose a cool name to call your cabin, pick a theme, draw a mascot, and have everyone in the bunk sign their names. Post it outside your bunk, and everyone at camp will know you're the friendliest group.

4. **Follow the rules.** Camps may have strict rules about what type of decorating is allowed, so be sure to follow all of the guidelines. Even if there aren't any rules, be sure that you don't damage the camp property. For example, don't carve your name into the bedpost or write on the walls. You know, the stuff that would get you in trouble at home.

Sleep Tight

Sleep may not be easy the first couple of nights. You may be excited, nervous, or simply adjusting to a new bed.

1. **Prepare your sleeping area early in the day.**
   The last thing you want to do is search for your sheets or find your pillow at the end of the day when you're tired. This is especially true if you are tent-camping, as you might not be able to find your belongings if it is dark or raining out.

2. **Go to bed as scheduled (as best as you can).** Your camp counselor will probably tell you when it is time to stop talking and turn out the lights. If you get a good night's sleep, you'll have the energy you need to get through the next day. If you "pull an all-nighter," staying up all night to tell stories, sing songs, and talk with your friends, you will have trouble staying focused the next day. Chances are, you'll have a late night or two, but do your best to get a good night's sleep.

3. **Shhh...** If you decide to stay up late, be sure to be respectful of others in the area who might want to sleep. If you are having trouble sleeping, read a book, write a letter, or do some other quiet activity.

Top and Bottom Bunk Pros and Cons

Many times, you are assigned to a cabin, but not a particular bed. This means you have the opportunity to choose a top or bottom bunk. Which one to choose? Hmmm....

TOP BUNK

Pros

You avoid having people sit easily on your bed.

People can't bump into you when they walk by.

You can write or read in private.

Cons

It might be difficult to climb up into bed.

Changing the sheets is tough.

Getting to the bathroom at 2 a.m. is tricky.

Watch your head—some top bunks
are very close to the ceiling!

BOTTOM BUNK

Pros

You can store shoes and other items on the floor under the bed.

You don't need to climb up and down the ladder.

You can play cards or other games with the other "bottom bunkers."

Cons

People are likely to sit down on your bed when they come in the room.

Any motion the top-bunker above you makes is disruptive.

You have less privacy.

37

Keep in Touch

At some point, your counselor will probably say, "OK, everybody. It's time to write home!" You may be thinking, "Oh no! It's my summer vacation and I have to *write*?" Take it easy, these letters won't be graded by any teachers and actually can be fun to write! Writing letters to your family and friends back home is a great way to share all of the exciting things you are doing at camp. This section has tips, tricks, and ideas to make the letters you write from camp easy to write and fun to read!

Before you leave for camp (and after you're sure you have packed enough underwear), be sure to pack the following letter-writing basics:

* Pens or pencils, paper, envelopes, and stamps. Take a few colored pens and some different types of paper so that your letters will be unique. Your camp will probably have extra paper and pens you can use for your letters, but it's always better to be prepared. Pack a box of crayons to make your letters extra colorful.

* Ask an adult to help you put addresses and the correct number of stamps on the envelopes before you leave. This will ensure your letters get to the right places. Pack all of these things in a safe spot so that you will be able to find them. In fact, you can even use the handy pocket at the back of this book to store everything you need for letter writing.

* You can also use the "Addresses" section at the back of this book to write some of your family members' and friends' addresses. But be sure to leave enough room to write down the addresses of all the cool friends you're going to make at camp.

Whom Should I Write To?

Everyone at home, of course! They'll all be excited to hear about the cool stuff you've been doing at camp, like canoeing, climbing on a ropes course, or tie-dyeing T-shirts. This includes grandparents, aunts, uncles, cousins, babysitters, or friends from school.

What Should I Write About?

As soon as camp gets started, there will be plenty for you to write about! A good letter from camp will also include things like:

* Who your counselor is, and what he or she is like.
* Names of your bunkmates, and how cool they are.
* How good or bad the food is.
* Any new skills you've learned, such as archery, new swimming strokes, or how to paddle a canoe.

 ## What if I'm Going to a Day Camp?

If you are going to day camp, this doesn't mean you can't write a letter about all of the fun you're having. You just have to be creative with how you do it. For example, when you get home from a day of camp, write a letter about all the great things you did that day. Write about your friends, swimming lessons, sports you played well, and songs you sang. Put this into Mom or Dad's lunch bag, pocket, or briefcase the next day, or leave it in a place you know they will find it. Or, you may have family members who live far away and who would love to hear about your adventures. Getting a letter from you will make their day and show them that you are having a fantastic summer.

Get Creative!

Now it's time to have some fun and write some awesome letters. Here are some ways to make yours unique and memorable:

Trace your hand or foot onto a piece of paper. Cut it out and write the letter on it. Include how tired your feet are from doing so many great activities.

* Find a flower, and send it wrapped up in your letter. Be sure to ask permission before picking any flowers at camp. Include in your letter a poem that thanks your parents for letting you go to camp.

* If you don't feel like writing a letter, draw one instead. You can make a slide show or comic strip of your favorite things at camp.

* If you plan on sending a letter to a friend, include a secret message using a code that they will have to figure out. To make a code, assign a symbol or number to each letter of the alphabet, and use these symbols to write your letter. Be sure to send a copy of the code with your letter so that your friend will be able to figure it out. Here's a simple code you can use:

A	B	C	D	E	F	G	H	I	J
1	2	3	4	5	6	7	8	9	10

K	L	M	N	O	P	Q	R	S	T
11	12	13	14	15	16	17	18	19	20

U	V	W	X	Y	Z
21	22	23	24	25	26

Can you figure out this sample message?

(3, 1, 13, 16) (18, 21, 12, 5, 19)

See below for answer.

Answer to the secret code: **Camp Rules!**

* You can make your letter look like ancient parchment: Rip the edges, stain the paper with coffee or tea, or rub dirt on it to make it looked old, cracked, and yellowing.

* To give yourself a challenge, try writing a letter without using a particular letter of the alphabet. Before you sit down to write, pick a letter to avoid using in your entire letter, such as the letter "e." For example, instead of writing "This camp is really awesome," write "This camp is lots of fun!" Or you can omit the letter in each word that uses it. For example, "This camp is rally awsom."

* Before you mail your letter, take some time to decorate the outside of the envelope. Draw pictures of canoes, sailboats, campfires, tents, and cabins to give your letter a camp-like look.

* Draw a diagram of your day at camp! First, draw a ground plan map of your campgrounds. It doesn't have to be accurate. In fact, you can draw your favorite spots bigger than the other places on your map. On your map, retrace your steps throughout the day, places such as the lake or pool, baseball field, arts and crafts cabin, and archery field. Draw pictures that illustrate what happened during the day in the locations where these events happened.

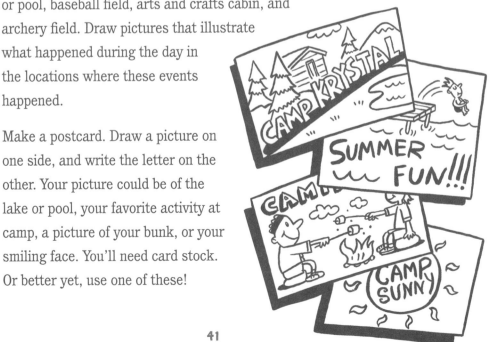

* Make a postcard. Draw a picture on one side, and write the letter on the other. Your picture could be of the lake or pool, your favorite activity at camp, a picture of your bunk, or your smiling face. You'll need card stock. Or better yet, use one of these!

PERFORATED
POSTCARDS

Just punch 'em out,
fill 'em in,
and mail 'em home!

CHAPTER 5

THE GREAT OUTDOORS

Everything You Need to Know about Playing Outside!

Prep Yourself for the Wilderness

Building forts, going on nature hikes, making campfires, and sleeping under the stars are some of the best parts about being outdoors. Sometimes you may have to deal with getting a little dirty, annoying bugs and other critters, and braving the heat of the summer sun. If you don't like this kind of thing, then you should choose camp activities that are mostly indoors. But if you enjoy outdoor adventures and wild experiences, then this section is for you!

Let's take a look at some of the things you'll encounter during your outdoor excursions.

WARNING!

After reading this chapter, you may be able to amaze your counselors and fellow campers with your incredible knowledge of the outdoors.

Dirt Don't Hurt!

et's face it. When you play outside, there's a chance you are going to get dirty. It's like having a Popsicle on a hot day: You know your fingers are going to get covered in sticky goo, but it doesn't stop you from eating that Popsicle, does it?

The fact is dirt really will not hurt you. But being prepared for it is the key. When you get ready to go to camp, it's a good idea to wear clothing and shoes that you don't mind getting a little dirty. These clothes and shoes should also help to keep you from getting hurt. For example, sandals and other open-toed footwear may be great at the beach, but exposed toes can be injured by twigs or rocks that get mixed in with the dirt at camp. Wearing long pants and long-sleeved shirts will help to keep you safe from bug and tick bites.

THE OLE SWIMMIN' HOLE

Most camps will have some type of swimming program as part of their daily activities. Though some camps have pools, many still rely on ponds and lakes that nature has provided. You may be a first-timer to swimming in a pond or a lake, and you'll find it's a little bit different from swimming in a pool.

Things Overheard by First-Timers to the Ole Swimmin' Hole

"I can't see my feet!" You will most likely not be able to see the bottom in many parts of a lake or pond. Because lakes and ponds are homes to many types of plants and animals, the water is usually darker than what you'll find in a pool. This does not mean that the lake or pond is dirty or unsafe. However, since you can't see to the bottom, be sure to check with the lifeguards about the water's depth before you swim in it.

"What about fish?" Fish, insects, frogs, spiders, and even snakes call a pond or a lake home. Be aware that you may come across some of these critters while you are swimming. If one happens to cross your path, the most important thing to do is relax. Do *not* panic. If you leave them alone, more often than not, they will leave you alone. Remember, you are swimming in their home, and they may just be curious about you.

"The water is so cold!" Chances are pretty good that the lake or pond water will be a little cooler than pool water. A pond or a lake is usually bigger than a pool, and there's much more water for the sun to heat up. Some ponds and lakes get water from springs that are under the ground, which can be chilly since the water hasn't been warmed by the sun at all.

"The ground is soft and squishy!" The bottom of a lake or pond is soil with lots of decomposing, organic matter (that's stuff that used to be alive). It's mostly just leaves and plants, but it makes the bottom squish between your toes. It may take a little getting used to, but it's not at all unhealthy or unsafe. Some camps add beach sand to their swimming areas to make it feel a bit more comfortable.

"Why do I have icky goo all over me after I get out?" Once again, you can blame that organic matter. In this case, it's probably a plant called "algae." Algae can grow just about anywhere there is water, and it serves as a food source for some animals. At certain times, like after a rain storm, the algae gets stirred up and sticks to your body when you swim. Don't worry, you can rinse it off when you come out of the water.

Swim Safely

Always swim with a buddy and make sure there is at least one lifeguard on duty before you enter the water.

TAKE A HIKE!

One of the most popular of all the outdoor activities is hiking. It's easy to do, it's great exercise, and it doesn't require any expensive equipment. Hiking can be done just about anywhere, and at many summer camps it is part of the daily program.

To be a responsible hiker, you'll need to follow some simple rules:

1. **YOU TAKE BACK FROM THE HIKE WHAT YOU TAKE ON THE HIKE. That means that whatever you take with you, especially trash from lunches, should come back with you so that you can dispose of it properly.**

2. **STAY ON THE TRAILS. Many places that are popular for hiking will have trails for you to follow. It is important always to stay on the trails. This will help you to avoid getting lost and will ensure that the least damage is done to the area.**

3. **STAY TOGETHER. Nobody should hike alone. Always hike with a buddy or a group, and be sure that every member of the hiking party knows where you are going and how to return to where you started.**

4. **AVOID TOUCHING ANY PLANTS OR ANIMALS YOU MAY ENCOUNTER. Some plants can cause allergic reactions to your skin, making you itchy, and any animal you see on a hike is wild. Wild animals should not be approached or touched. Remember, you are walking through their home, and you should respect them.**

Getting ready for a hike depends on where and how far you are going, what type of terrain, or ground, you will be walking on, and how long you plan to be out on your hike. Some hikes last a few hours. Some can last a few days. When you know what kind of a hike you will be taking, you can use this list to make sure you are completely prepared.

* Bring plenty of water. Avoid bringing drinks like soda. You need to keep your body well hydrated, meaning you should have enough healthy stuff to drink to help your body work well.

* Wear comfortable shoes, like hiking boots or sneakers. Think about your toes before you plan on wearing sandals.

* Put on sunscreen before your hike, and have some extra handy.

* Wear a hat.

* Keep a flashlight in your pack, especially if you are planning a night hike. Double-check that it works before you leave, and bring an extra set of batteries, just in case.

* Wear and bring insect repellant.

* Pack raingear or a trash-bag poncho, which works just as well.

* Practice how to whistle. This can be used as a signal if you need help or to scare off animals.

* Your counselor or group leader should carry a first aid kit and any medications you may need. But it doesn't hurt to bring your own adhesive bandages along if you have them.

* Bring food. It's important to give your body enough energy for the hike. Don't skip out on breakfast on the day of your hike, and bring some food with you if you'll be out all day.

* Carry a trail map and field guides if they are available. When you step onto a trail for the first time, you may see plants and animals that you have not seen before. A field guide will help you to identify what you are seeing and can make the hike much more enjoyable.

* If you have a compass and know how to use it, bring it along. (To learn more about using a compass, see section "Using a Compass, the Basics" on page 58.)

* A disposable camera is great for hikes. They aren't heavy, and they don't cost a lot of money in the event that they get ruined or lost.

* Only pack things that are necessary for the hike. CD players or other electronic devices will make your backpack heavy and can get broken along the way.

* Always hike with at least one other person. At camp, you should be with your counselor and other campers at all times.

* Before you leave tell someone where you are going, what time you are leaving, and what time you plan to come back.

A hike doesn't have to be just a walk in the woods. There are many different ways to make a hike more fun. You are limited only by your imagination. Here are some different types of hikes you can take:

Night Hike. Grab a flashlight and take a hike at night! Be sure to go as a group and stay together with your counselor or bunk leader. Frequently take breaks, and

check to make sure everyone is with the group. A fun way to keep track of everyone is to give each person in the group a number. When your leader shouts, "Count off," everyone says their number out loud and in number order. If one of the numbers is missing, you'll know a camper is missing.

Scavenger Hunt Hike. Before you begin your hike, make a list of things you will need to find. The list can include things like sticks in the shapes of letters, rocks that are round, three different kinds of leaves, or the biggest acorn you can find. Only collect items that you find on the ground. Do not remove any living item, like flowers, from the forest or break off any live tree branches—things that live and grow in the woods should stay there. If you want to include items like these, it is a good idea to make it a rule to write a description of the item and its location, instead of removing it.

Nature Hike. Notice different types of plants and animals as you enjoy your walk through the woods. If you have a field guide, use it to identify some of the different plants and animals you see. If not, keep track of the different plants and animals you come across. Pack some binoculars if you have them, and be a good observer.

I-Spy Hike. As you hike along the trails, one person chooses something specific that can be seen up ahead, like an interesting tree or a huge rock. Then the rest of the group asks questions about the object that can only be answered with "yes" or "no." The group must try to guess what the object is before they pass it. If the group cannot guess the object, the chooser reveals what it is. Choose another object and the game continues. If someone in the group guesses the object before it is passed, then that person gets to choose the next object for the group to ask questions about.

Activity: Make a Trash Bag Poncho!

(Adult Supervision Required)

Turn a trash bag upside down so that you are grabbing the bottom with your hands. Cut out a hole in the middle at the top for your head and two holes on either side to fit your arms through. Now you have a homemade poncho.

Don't Let the Bugs Bug You!

Bugs are an everyday part of outdoor activities, and they will be a part of your camp experience. If you have ever spent time in your own yard, at a picnic, in the park, or camping with your family, then you've probably noticed that bugs, particularly the flying ones, can be a pain. Mosquitoes, black flies, bees, and ticks are attracted to people for many different reasons. Here are some tips for keeping them away:

1. Avoid wearing brightly colored clothing and anything with a pattern that looks like flowers. Stinging insects, like bees, are attracted to them.

2. Stay away from areas where the grass is high and wet, and places where there is standing water (like a puddle). Mosquitoes will commonly be found there.

3. When you dress for the outdoors, especially for hiking through the woods, wear light-colored clothing that covers most of your body. Long-sleeve shirts and pants will give you more protection from biting and stinging insects, and mosquitoes are not attracted to light colors such as khaki, beige, or olive. These colors will also make it easier to notice any ticks on your clothing.

4. Avoid wearing perfume or sweet-smelling fragrances. These will attract insects to you.

5. Don't leave your food or drink uncovered for too long. Insects, especially bees, are attracted to sweet foods and drinks.

6. Don't swat at bees if they come near you, because this may encourage them to sting you. If you do get stung by a bee, let your counselor or group leader know immediately.

7. Be very careful when you use insect repellant. Spray it only onto your clothing, and never near your eyes or mouth. Be sure to read the can and follow all of the instructions.

Wanna Hear Something Cool?
Mosquitoes are attracted to the carbon dioxide we breathe out.

A Little Bit about Ticks

Ticks are little, dark-colored arachnids. Like a spider, adult ticks have eight legs. They are commonly found in wooded areas and grassy fields, especially in New England and parts of the Midwest. Ticks cannot jump, so they crawl onto people when they brush up against tall grasses or other plants. This is why it is important to stay on properly cleared trails when hiking through the woods. Ticks attach themselves to people and animals and bite them. If you get bitten by a tick, you probably won't feel anything, but they feed on blood when they are attached to an animal. This is why it is important to check yourself and others each time you walk or play in the woods. If you see a tick on your clothing, or find that you have been bitten, let your counselor or group leader know right away.

LEAVES OF THREE...LET IT BE!

This may be one of the most important rules to remember when enjoying the outdoors. Certain plants like poison ivy, poison sumac, and poison oak can leave you with a nasty rash if you touch them. These plants will have three leaves on each stem. Count the leaves of any plant, and use the rule of three to find poison ivy, which can grow as a bush, a vine, or individual plants, and poison oak, which grows as a thick bush. Poison sumac grows in standing water near swamps and may have as many as 13 leaves on a stem. See the pictures below to help you identify these rash-inducing plants.

Poison ivy, poison oak, or poison sumac can be found in every one of the United States, except Alaska and Hawaii. If you are careful when outdoors, you should be able to avoid these plants.

Poison Ivy

Poison Oak

Poison Sumac

What Causes the Itch?

These plants have an oil in them called "urushiol" (pronounced u-roo-she-all), which can get onto your clothing or skin when you touch these plants. If you know you have touched poison ivy, poison oak, or poison sumac, the best way to prevent getting a rash is to take a hot shower as soon as possible. Any clothing, shoes, sports equipment, or other items that may have come into contact with these plants should be washed well with soap and water before they are used again.

Using a Compass, the Basics

A compass is an instrument that is used to find the direction you are traveling while hiking. It is important to know in what direction you are traveling in order to avoid getting lost. However, simply having a compass doesn't mean you won't get lost—you need to know how to use it. A compass will have a little red needle, which is actually a little magnet. It will always point north, because it is attracted to the Earth's magnetic North Pole.

To use a compass, you must know the four basic directions: north (N), south (S), east (E), and west (W).

Hold the compass in your hand. Make sure it is flat so that the arrow can turn easily. Wait until the needle has stopped moving. It should be pointing to the north. Try turning your body around. As long as the compass stays flat, the needle will always point to the north. To walk north, point your body in the direction that the red arrow is pointing and walk. To walk east, turn to your right to point your body in the direction of east and walk. The same method will work if you choose to walk south or west.

It's also important to know the area in which you plan to be traveling. If you can find a map of your hiking trail, bring it along.

ACTIVITY: COMPASS TREASURE HUNT

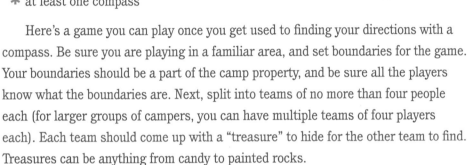

What each team will need:

* one "treasure"
* one flag; a bandana or other colored cloth will work
* some paper
* a pen or pencil
* at least one compass

Here's a game you can play once you get used to finding your directions with a compass. Be sure you are playing in a familiar area, and set boundaries for the game. Your boundaries should be a part of the camp property, and be sure all the players know what the boundaries are. Next, split into teams of no more than four people each (for larger groups of campers, you can have multiple teams of four players each). Each team should come up with a "treasure" to hide for the other team to find. Treasures can be anything from candy to painted rocks.

Choose which will be the "hiding" team, and which other team will be the "seekers." Once that's figured out, it's time to hide the treasure! The team that is hiding the treasure should pick a "starting point." From the starting point, the hiding team begins walking to the spot where they will hide the treasure. All members of any seeking teams should not be near the starting point yet. They should wait in another place like a bunk or at a picnic table away from the starting point. As the hiding team begins to walk to find a hiding spot, they should write down each of the directions they've traveled and the number of steps (paces) they've taken in each direction on their way there. These directions will lead the other teams to the treasure. As soon as the team has picked a good hiding spot, they should bury their treasure there. Place the flag at the spot where the treasure is buried so that the other teams will know they followed the directions correctly. Return to the starting point and hand over your directions to the team of seekers. If there is more than one team, make sure you have multiple copies of your directions, and the first team to find the treasure wins! Here is what your directions may look like:

1. Start by the old oak tree near the lake.
2. Walk 25 paces to the east.
3. Turn and walk 15 paces to the northwest.
4. You should be standing near Captain's Tree Stump.
5. From there, walk 18 paces to the northeast.
6. Take 21 paces to the southeast.
7. You should see three evergreen trees growing in a triangle.
8. From there, walk 35 paces to the north.
9. If you are in the right spot, you'll notice the white trail marker on a huge tree.
10. Walk 15 paces west.
11. Walk 10 more paces north.
12. Finally, walk 20 paces to the northwest.
13. Look around, our flag marks the spot!

Make the directions challenging, but fair. Lead them to the treasure, and not just in circles around the area.

What is the Earth's Magnetic North Pole?

Picture a huge magnet that runs through the core of the Earth from the south to the north. The North Pole's huge magnet attracts the smaller one (the needle) inside your compass. However, the magnetic North Pole is not located at the exact northern point of the Earth. It's actually located in the Queen Elizabeth Islands of extreme northern Canada, about 4 degrees south of the geographic North Pole, and it is slowly moving northwest. But for your purposes hiking with a compass, you won't be able to notice the difference between magnetic north and actual north.

CHAPTER 6

FUN ACTIVITIES & CLASSIC CAMP GAMES

Let's Play!

Fill-In-the-Blanks

our counselor will make sure that there are activities for you to do at camp, from arts and crafts to canoeing, field games to campfire cooking. However, the best times at camp often take place during the "down times," or the times when activities aren't planned. Get ready for some games to fill in your free time.

JOUSTING

Partners face each other and attempt to cause the other person to move his feet. The first person to cause the other person to move three times wins.

How to play:

1. Pick one partner and stand face-to-face with him.
2. Stand far enough apart that you can barely place your fingertips on the other person's shoulders, but don't hold on to the other person's shoulders.
3. You and your partner should stand with your legs closed and feet close together. Your feet must stay in this position for the game.
4. Both of you raise your hands to about chest level, with palms facing forward and arms slightly bent.
5. When both players are ready, start the game. Each player tries to push the palms of their opponent, in an attempt to cause him to lose his balance and move his feet.
6. You can take turns challenging different campers, or even have a jousting tournament.

Tip This is a game of strategy, not strength! For example, Player A pushes with all of his might, and Person B simply drops his hands, and then Player A will most likely fall forward.

TOE FENCING

Be the first to tag the other player's toes three times with your foot.

How to play:

1. Pick one partner, and stand face-to-face with her.
2. Be sure that both players have the same level of foot protection (bare foot to bare foot or shoe to shoe).
3. Stand far enough apart that you can put your hands on the other person's shoulders, and hold on firmly.
4. Try to tag the other player's feet without getting yours tagged. You will be hopping around a lot. Remember, you want to tag your opponent's feet, not stomp on them!
5. As soon as you've tapped your opponent's toes three times, she is out and a new person can play.

20 QUESTIONS

While asking twenty questions or less, guess the name of an object in plain sight that someone has chosen.

How to play:

1. One person silently chooses an object in plain sight of the group.
2. The rest of the players can then take turns asking questions that can only be answered "yes" or "no," until someone can correctly guess what the object is.
3. If someone correctly guesses the object before the twentieth question is asked, he is the next person to choose the object. If the group cannot guess correctly before they've asked twenty questions, the chooser tells what the object is and gets to choose again.

THE NEVER-ENDING STORY

Everyone pitches in to tell a great tall tale!

How to play:

1. Everyone should sit in a circle. One camper starts the story with an interesting sentence, such as "Last summer, I was hiking in the woods near my house and found the strangest thing!"

2. The next camper in the circle adds a new sentence that carries on the story.

3. Each camper adds a line when it's her turn. Campers can change the direction of the story any way they choose by adding funny or scary lines.

Rain, Rain, Don't Go Away

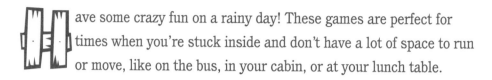

ave some crazy fun on a rainy day! These games are perfect for times when you're stuck inside and don't have a lot of space to run or move, like on the bus, in your cabin, or at your lunch table.

RHYTHM GAME

Guess who the leader of the band is.

How to play:

1. One person is chosen as the guesser and must leave the room or immediate area. Tell the guesser that when he comes back, the rest of the group will be performing a music show and that he must guess who the leader is.

2. The rest of the group sits in a circle. One of the people in the circle is chosen as the leader.

3. The leader begins to make a rhythm by clapping her hands, snapping her fingers, tapping her head, stomping her feet, or doing other actions. The rest of the group must follow the leader in whatever she does. The leader can change the actions whenever she chooses, and the rest of the group must follow along.

4. After a few practice rhythms, the group calls the guesser back to the circle.

5. The guesser has to observe the group and has three chances to correctly choose the leader.

Tip If everyone looks at the leader, it is very easy to figure out who the leader is. Only one or two people should look directly at the leader. Everyone else in the group should look at other people. As the leader changes motions, the motions will quickly pass from the people looking at the leader to the rest of the group.

SANDMAN (ALSO KNOWN AS "WINK OR SPY")

The Sandman is putting people to sleep!

How to play:

1. Everyone sits in a circle and closes their eyes.
2. One person (usually the counselor) will walk around the circle and choose one sandman and one detective out of the group by tapping two different campers on the head. The sandman is tapped once, and the detective is tapped twice.
3. As soon as the chooser sits back down, everyone opens their eyes and looks around the circle at the other players. The detective must announce himself, and then try to figure out who in the circle is the sandman, which is kept a secret.
4. The sandman's goal is to wink at people in the group to make them "fall asleep" without being seen by the detective.
5. Once the players are winked at by the sandman, they have to pretend to go to sleep. The players can really ham it up by taking a big yawn and stretching, and then putting their heads down.
6. The detective has three guesses to get it right or the sandman wins the round.

65

CELEBRITY NAME GAME

Pass the names of your favorite celebrities around the group without making a mistake.

How to play:

1. Everyone sits in a circle. If you are playing from your bunks or different spots on the bus, you should agree about the order in which everyone plays.

2. Choose one person to start the game. This person begins the game by calling out the name of a musician or an actor, for example, "Brad Pitt."

3. The next person continues the game by calling out a new celebrity whose name begins with the first letter of the previous celebrity's last name. "Brad Pitt" can be followed by "Paula Abdul," who could then be followed by "Adam Sandler."

4. If someone calls out a celebrity whose first and last names start with the same letter, the group should reverse the direction of play. For example, if player 1 calls out "John Lennon" and player 2 calls out "Lucy Liu," it would be player 1's turn again.

5. If a person calls out a celebrity who is known by one name, skip the next person in line. For example, if player 1 calls out "Tobey Maguire" and player 2 calls out "Madonna," then player 3 is skipped.

6. If the next person in line can't think of a name within five seconds, they are "out" and the next person gets a chance to call out a name.

7. The game continues until there is one person left. You can play the game with all celebrities, or choose a specific category, like "musicians" or "baseball players."

66

ALIEN LANGUAGE BRAINTEASER

Teach your friends how to count in a secret alien language.

How to play:

1. Explain to your friends that you were captured by aliens a long, long time ago. The only thing you remember from the experience is how to count from zero to ten in their alien language. Tell your friends that you are willing to show them the secret alien numbers, and give them a chance to learn it for themselves.

2. Next, arrange six sticks or pens in a pattern on the ground. Stand up, and cross your arms across your chest with authority. Tell the group that you are showing them a number between zero and ten and that they should try to guess the number you are showing. The pattern is completely random. In fact, the sticks have nothing to do with the actual number. Read on to learn the secret.

3. Tell them that once they discover the secret, they can't share it with others in the group, since everyone needs to figure it out for themselves.

4. Give everyone a few guesses, and then tell them the correct number. Put down another pattern, and try it again.

5. Ready for the secret? The way you cross your arms and show your fingers tells the players what the proper number is. For example, if you cross your arms and  rest all of your fingers on the outside of your arms, the correct number is ten. If you cross your arms and place three fingers from each hand on the outside of your arms, the number is a six. Pretty tricky, isn't it?

6. Repeat the process until everyone understands the game, or until everyone is frustrated and threatening to lock you outside of the cabin.

Tip Your friends will eventually begin to catch on. If no one discovers the secret right away, you can be more dramatic and obvious when you cross your arms.

Frisbee® Games

These games are simple and lots of fun. All you need to start is a Frisbee, a place where you can play that is free of obstacles (like a field), and players who are ready to run around and have some fun.

FRISBEE BOWLING

Frisbee bowling is similar to regular bowling. The object is to knock down as many pins as you can by throwing the Frisbee at them.

How to play:

1. Choose a playing field that is about 20 to 30 feet long. This will be your bowling alley.

2. Set up ten pins at one end. The pins can be any object that can stand on its own, but is light enough to be knocked over with a Frisbee. Set up the pins in a triangle that is made up of four rows. Put one pin in the first row, two pins side-by-side in the second row, three pins side-by-side in the third row, and four pins side-by side in the fourth row. It will look something like this:

3. Each player takes a turn throwing the Frisbee at the pins. Each round will consist of two throws per player. Count the number of pins you knock over on the first throw, and add them to the number of pins you knock over on the second throw. That is your score for the round. The best score a player can get with two throws is a ten. If you knock down all the pins on the first throw, the round is over and you get a score of eleven.

4. After each person plays ten rounds, add up your score. The player with the most pins knocked over wins.

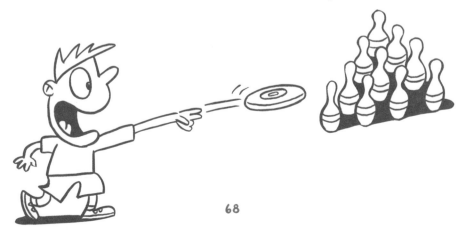

ULTIMATE FRISBEE, AKA "ULTIMATE"

In recent years, this has become the most popular Frisbee game. It is similar to football, except Ultimate Frisbee is a *non-contact game.* This means there is no tackling. You will need a large, flat field and at least eight to ten players to play this game. The object is to score a goal by throwing the Frisbee to a player on your team while he is in the other team's end zone.

How to play:

1. A regulation playing area is 70 yards long and 40 yards wide, but you can play the game on any flat, grassy field that is free of dangerous obstructions, like trees. Set up two end zones opposite from each other at the ends of the playing area. These can be marked by cones or any other object that can be seen easily. Make each end zone about 20 to 30 feet wide. Determine the limits of your game: how much time do you want your game to last, or will you play to a certain point level? Once that's decided, designate a time keeper or a score keeper.

2. Form two teams of up to eleven players each. Both teams stand in front of their own end zone.

3. Choose which team will throw off the Frisbee to begin the game. A good way to do this is a Frisbee toss. Each team chooses a side of the Frisbee just like in a coin toss. For example, Team A chooses the side with the logo or picture (the top), and Team B chooses the bottom. The Frisbee is flipped into the air. If it lands with the logo or picture facing up, Team A will get to choose if they want to "throw off" the Frisbee or receive the Frisbee at the start of the game.

4. To begin the game, the team designated to "throw off" will throw the Frisbee across the field to the other team.

5. The team that catches the Frisbee will try to advance down the field toward the end zone they are facing by throwing and catching the Frisbee between the teammates. Players cannot run while holding the Frisbee, and they must throw the Frisbee to another teammate within ten seconds of catching it.

6. A team can score a goal if one teammate passes the Frisbee into the end zone to another teammate who catches it. After a score, both teams go back to the sides of the field on which they began for a "throw off." The team that just scored will throw the Frisbee to the other team.

7. When your team does not have the Frisbee, you are on defense. Your job is to try to knock the Frisbee out of the air during a pass or to intercept the Frisbee and catch it yourself. When defending against a thrower (a person who has the Frisbee), you may stand in front of him or her, but you must give them some room to throw. If you are not guarding the thrower, keep an eye out for the other players. Stay near them. If the Frisbee is thrown to them, you may have a chance to intercept it.

8. Possession of the Frisbee changes if a player drops it, misses catching it, it goes out of bounds, or it is intercepted by the other team. For example, if your teammate passes you the Frisbee and you miss it, the other team gets possession of the Frisbee and your team becomes the defense.

9. The team with the most points at the end of the time limit, or the team that reaches the pre-determined point limit wins!

Ultimate Frisbee® Strategies

1. Try to spread out during the game. Don't go too far though—short passes are easier to handle.

2. If you don't have the Frisbee, but one of your teammates does, try moving away from the person defending against you in a zigzag, until it's clear for your teammate to throw the Frisbee to you.

3. On defense, if the Frisbee is passed to a player near you, but you don't think you can catch it, just try to knock it down. As long as the other team does not catch it, possession of the Frisbee will change and you or one of your teammates can pick it up.

FRISBEE GOLF

Frisbee golf is similar to regular golf. The object is to hit a target in the fewest number of Frisbee throws. It can be played alone or in groups of up to four people at a time. If there is more than one group of players, let one group begin. When they are safely out of the way, the next group may begin.

How to play:

1. Choose "tees," the spots where the Frisbee will be thrown from, and "holes," the spots that will be targets. The targets can be as simple as a tree or a rock, but be sure only to choose targets that will not be damaged by the Frisbee. The course can be planned out so that each hole ends near the next tee. Choose as many holes as you'd like, from nine to 18.

2. Each player takes a turn throwing the Frisbee from the tee. Each throw equals one "stroke," just like on a golf course. On a piece of paper, mark down each stroke it takes for a player to hit each target "hole."

3. After you play through all the "holes," add up the scores. The player with the lowest score wins.

Camp Classics

Every camp has favorite games that its campers enjoy playing. Some are made up at the camp, or are just popular there. These games, however, are camp *classics*, and hardly a camp exists without them!

CAPTURE THE FLAG

Camp just wouldn't be camp without a few games of Capture the Flag. The best part of the game isn't the strategy, the exciting jail breaks, or bringing the flag over the safety line—it's the victory lap through camp with your rival's flag held high that makes it all worth it!

A Quick Overview

Capture the Flag is a hunt-and-find game that combines hide-and-seek with tag. Two teams are given equal-size playing areas that serve as the team's "zone," such as one-half of a ball field or a large area of woods. Each team has a flag it must guard in its zone. The goal of the game is to find the other team's flag, capture it (steal it), and return it to your zone without getting tagged. There are generally ten to 40 players on each side, although you could play with as few as five players per side.

What you will need:
* one watch per team
* something to be the flag; a bandana, towel, sweatshirt, or other brightly colored material
* branch or stake, to hold the flag up in the air
* backpacks, towels, and other things to serve as a boundary

How to play:

1. **SETTING UP THE ZONES: Many camps use orange cones or camp landmarks to set up the boundaries of the playing area. The playing areas could be a ball field, a section of woods, or even the whole camp. The teams should divide the playing area in half in one of two ways:**
   - ◉ Spread out a series of items, such as book bags or towels, on the ground in a straight line across the middle of the area to serve as the dividing line. This technique is most often used when the playing area is in a ball field.
   - ◉ Use an established hiking trail as the dividing line when you're playing in a wooded area. Your counselors should review the playing area with you.
   - ◉ Each team must section off an area in its zone to be used as a jail. You can use a rope, branches, or even imaginary boundaries between a couple of trees. The jails are usually located midway between the boundaries of a team's side, as far away from the flag as possible; however, you can put your jail wherever you like. Teams are not required to tell the other team where the jail is located if it is not in plain view.

2. **HIDING THE FLAG: Each team creates its own flag by placing a towel, bandana, or any brightly colored piece of fabric on top of a large stake or branch inserted into the ground in that team's zone. Usually, the flag is not visible from the other team's** zone, but must be visible from ten feet away, so you can't cover it with a bag or hide it directly behind a tree.

3. **STARTING THE GAME: The teams meet in the center of the playing area and review the boundaries and the rules. As soon as this is done, the teams have five minutes to set up their side. At the end of the five minutes, the teams are allowed to begin the game. Be sure to bring your watch! Generally, the start of the game is on the honor system, but your camp may have a bell or whistle to start the game.**

4. **CAPTURING THE FLAG: Members of your team must cross into the other team's zone, find their flag, grab it, and bring it back to any part of your zone without getting tagged. If you capture the flag and get tagged, you must go to jail, and the flag is returned to its original spot.**

5. **PROTECTING YOUR FLAG: While you are in your team's zone, you are safe from capture. Once an opponent dares to cross onto your zone (called "crossing enemy lines"), you can tag your opponent and bring him or her to your team's "jail" as your prisoner. Remember, the same can be done to you if you cross into your opponent's zone.**

6. **JAIL: Prisoners must wait in jail until the game ends or they are set free, as described in the following "Jail Breaks" section. Be sure to assign a player or two to serve as jail guards to tag opponents who approach your jail or your prisoners. Jail guards wait in front of the jail area and**

watch carefully for members of the opposing team. If any players from the opposing team approach and try to free the prisoners, as described in the next section, the jail guards try to tag them.

7. JAIL BREAKS: One of the best twists to Capture the Flag is a jail break. If you are captured, you are sent to the jail in the opposing team's zone, where you can shout for help while you wait to be rescued. To escape from jail, a member of your team must cross over enemy lines, sneak past the jail guards, and tag you. Once you are tagged, you are free. You must return to your zone before you try to capture the flag again. You are allowed "free walk backs" to your side after a jail break, and are immune from capture while you return to your team's side.

8. WINNING THE GAME: Before the game begins, the teams agree on a set amount of time to play (generally about an hour). The team that captures the other team's flag first wins. If a flag is captured early in the hour, teams can declare a rematch and play until time runs out. In the event of multiple rematches, the team with the most flag captures before the time runs out wins.

Capture the Flag Strategies

Creating the perfect master plan is the key to winning Capture the Flag. Here are some proven strategies you can suggest to your team:

* **Border Patrol:** Assign players to protect the dividing line between zones. These players always stay in their zone, and their only job is to tag opponents when they first cross enemy lines or while they try to return to their *own* zone.

* **Look-outs:** Hide a player or two whose only job is to alert jail and flag guards of approaching opponents.

* **Wave Attacks:** Send a small group of two or more players (called a "wave") to try to capture the flag. Once the other team's flag guards are chasing them, a second wave runs in and captures the flag. You can use this same strategy for jail breaks.

KICK THE CAN

Players must kick the can without being caught by the guard!

A Quick Overview

Kick the Can combines elements of Hide and Seek, Tag, and Capture the Flag. One person is chosen as the "guard" of the can, and he must protect the can for the entire game. The guard is responsible for finding hiding players and preventing them from kicking the can. The rest of the players hide within the designated playing area and make attempts to kick the can without being caught by the guard. If the guard catches one of the players sneaking up to kick the can, he can send that player to jail. The game officially ends when the guard has caught all of the players and sent them to jail. This is a great game that can be played in rounds repeatedly until everyone is ready to stop.

Over the Can

In Kick the Can, the guard does not tag other players with his hands, but goes "over the can" on them. Remember this phrase because it's very important. In order to catch a player and send them to jail, the guard only needs to see them, call out "over the can on (insert name of player)," and jump over the can. Once he does this, the player must report directly to jail.

If the guard finds multiple players hiding next to each other or charging the can at the same time, he must call "over the can" and call out the names of each player, and jump over the can that many times. For example: The guard cannot call out, "over the can on Bob, Sara, Jose, and Elly," and jump over the can just once—he has to jump over the can four times.

The Perfect Can

A recycled soda or water bottle with a twist top is a good "can." Fill the empty bottle with an inch of sand or pebbles, and screw the top on tightly. This will help the can go farther when kicked, and will keep it from falling over on windy days.

How to play:

1. Define your playing area. This game is best played in a field with lots of things to hide behind, such as trees, sheds, or playground equipment.

2. Establish a "jail" area. You can use a bench, picnic table, or a space between a couple of book bags. People who are caught will sit in jail until another player kicks the can. The jail is typically 20 feet or so from the can.

3. Choose a guard. This person will be responsible for finding all the hiding players before they sneak up and kick the can.

4. Have all players make a circle and call out their name one by one. This is most important for the guard, who will need to identify players by name in order to catch them. This helps if you are playing with campers from other groups, or if you play before everyone knows each other really well.

5. The guard draws a circle in the dirt and puts the can inside it, then moves a few feet away from the bottle.

6. One of the players (but not the guard) kicks the can away from the circle to start the game.

7. The guard must run and return the can to its original spot, then close his eyes and count to 20 very loudly and slowly.

8. While the guard is retrieving the can and counting to 20, all the other players run and hide.

9. As soon as the guard stops counting, he may open his eyes and begin to look for other players. This is where the real action begins!

10. As soon as the guard opens his eyes, any number of the following actions may occur:

- The guard finds players who are hiding and goes "over the can" on them to send them to jail.
- Players leave their hiding spots and attempt to kick the can before the guard can go "over the can" on them.
- The guard goes "over the can" on a player charging the can before he can kick it and sends that player to jail.
- A player kicks the can successfully without being caught. Everyone in jail goes free, and the guard sets up the can and starts counting to 20 again to begin another round.

11. Generally, the guard tries as quickly as possible to find players who are not hidden well, and go "over the can" on them.

12. Once those players are sent to jail, the guard should move farther away from the can to find the other players. At this point, it's easier for players to leave their hiding spots and try to kick the can.

13. If a player leaves his hiding spot and successfully kicks the can without being caught, everyone in jail goes free.

- If a player leaves his hiding spot, and the guard notices and is able to successfully go "over the can" before the player can kick it, that player is out and must go to jail. Be careful to avoid a collision if the player is charging the can while the guard is attempting to jump over it!

14. To keep the game fresh and fun, especially for the guard, you can have a "two-can" rule. If two players are able to kick the can, the guard leaves his post, and the first person sent to jail becomes the new guard.

Kick the Can Strategies

If you are not the guard:

* **Try to plan your hiding spot with another player.** If one or two players hide close to the can, they can charge the can when the guard leaves his post.

* **Use the jailhouse snitches.** Players in jail are near the can and the guard. If the prisoners can signal to other players that the guard is far away from the can, they can charge the can without getting caught.

* **Charge the can in waves.** If two or more people go to kick the can at once, it will be very hard for the guard to successfully call "over the can," on each player and jump several times before someone can kick the can.

If you are the guard:

* **Expand your search area slowly.** Start by looking for players near the can by turning around in a circle slowly. When you need to search farther away from the can, move quickly to a new distance, look around, and run back to the can.

* **Learn to look behind a hiding spot.** A good way to do this is to approach it backward with your body facing the can. This way, you can scan for players around the can. More importantly, if someone runs out from behind the hiding spot you are approaching, you don't have to turn around to run back to the can. Very sneaky.

FOUR SQUARE

One Square, Two Square, Three Square... Four!

You may have played this game at school, but it's also very popular at camp. Players use their hands to hit a ball into other players' squares. If a player cannot return a ball hit into their square, he or she is out of the game. The squares are numbered 1 to 4, with square 4 being the most valuable one to be standing in. The goal is to move from the first square to the fourth square by trying to remove the players in the higher-value squares.

What you will need:

* Chalk or masking tape to set up a four-square court. (A four-square court is one large square divided into four smaller squares, and each smaller square is about 6 feet wide on each side. Your camp may already have an official court. Each square is assigned a number: 1, 2, 3, and 4.)

* A kickball, or other rubber playground ball.

How to play:

1. At the beginning of the game, there are only four players on the court, and they take any square they want, on a first-come first-serve basis. Generally, when your counselor says, "Let's play Four Square!" everyone scrambles to be the first one to step into and claim square 4. Additional players will stand in line a few feet away from the court and wait their turn to join the game.

2. The person in square 4 serves the first play by bouncing the ball once in their square, and then hitting it directly into any other player's square.

3. When a ball is hit into your square, you must hit it into another player's square before it bounces again, similar to a tennis volley.

4. The game goes on like this until one player either hits it outside the lines of another player's box (out of bounds) or is unable to return a ball hit in his square before the second bounce. The player who makes the mistake is out of the game, and must get in line behind the other waiting players. The next player in line takes her place in the empty square.

5. You are also out of the game if you hit the ball before it bounces in your square.

6. When players in squares 2 to 4 are out, the players rotate to the square with the next-higher number. For example, if the player in square 4 is out, the player in square 3 moves to square 4, the player in square 2 moves to square 3, and the player in square 1 moves to square 2. A new player from the waiting line then enters square 1.

7. The ultimate goal is to move your way into square 4, which is the best spot in the game. The player in square 4 always gets to serve the ball and is allowed to make special rules of the round (see box on next page).

8. Since players are always rotating into play, the game continues until it is time to move onto another activity. It is not uncommon to play Four Square for hours!

Some Other Ways to Play Four Square

These are the basic rules to Four Square: one bounce, one hit. Each time the ball is served, the person in square 4 calls out the special rules for the round. There are tons of rules that the player in square 4 can create:

✳ **Double Taps.** When a ball bounces in your square, you may hit it once into the air, above your head, and then once more into another player's square.

✳ **Bus Stops.** You are allowed to hit the ball into another player's square before it hits the ground in your box.

✳ **Showdown.** The player in square 4 calls "Showdown" between two squares before serving, and just the players in those squares can hit the ball between each other until one of the two messes up and is out. For example, if square 4 called "Showdown between 1 and 3!" only the players is squares 1 and 3 can hit the ball between each other until one of them is out.

✳ **Force Field.** The person in square 4 calls "Force field" on a square other than square 4, and any player who hits the ball into that square is out. This is a good rule to help out a first-time player who is having bad luck getting past square 1.

✳ **Announcements.** The person in square 4 calls "Announcements" and a category, such as "TV shows." The players must announce something from that category before they hit the ball.

COLOR GAMES

Color Games is one of the best traditions of summer camp! Imagine every moment of camp turned into a contest. Imagine becoming a hero in the eyes of your fellow teammates because you made the loudest armpit noises or ate the most pudding. Imagine an opposing team member winning ten points for wearing all red clothes and you scoring 20 points because you painted your entire body blue.

Color Games is a spirit competition that sometimes lasts all season. The entire camp is divided into four teams, each with campers of every age. It's called "Color Games" because the team names are usually colors, like Red, Yellow, Blue, and Green. Neutral judges, such as the camp director and camp nurse, award points throughout each day. You earn these points by winning contests, singing songs, performing skits, and having outstanding team spirit. The team with the most points at the end of the session wins.

Teams compete in a wide range of fun events, such as three-legged races, obstacle courses, and relay races. Almost every event can be turned into a contest for points, and everybody gets to participate, so Color Games days are extra fun! Below are some common contest categories and sample events. Be sure to read the "Do's and Don'ts" section below for tips on perfecting your performance in all categories.

Athletic events are perfect for the sports-minded camper: relay races, swim races, push-up or pull-up contests, and throwing a football or Frisbee for accuracy are just some of the challenging events that await you in this category.

Non-athletic events are fun activities designed to focus more on teamwork or individual talents. These may include cup stacking, pie-eating, spitting watermelon seeds for distance, garbage collecting, and scavenger hunts.

Team-spirit points are won by demonstrating that you think your team is the best. Teams can win points by wearing a particular color, creatively decorating their campsite or cabin in the team color, or performing camp community service. Part of team spirit includes appreciation for your opponents, so be sure your display of spirit doesn't ruin anyone else's fun.

Songs and chants are a very important Color Games tradition. Teams chant or sing songs throughout the day at camp to keep their teammates energized. Some of these songs and chants can be created by your own team. The judges give points for the best team chant and song of the day.

Skits and talent shows are another way for your team to impress the judges. Throughout the session, your team will put on many skits and performances for the rest of the camp. Judges will award points based on how funny or interesting they thought your performance was, and how well your act represented your team color and the values of your camp.

DO's and DON'Ts of Color Games

Remember, Color Games is a camp-spirit competition, and it's meant to be fun and fair. Team spirit and a positive attitude will help you get an edge over your competitors. Here are some great tips:

DO be a good sport. Clap and cheer for competitors, play fair in all contests, and always try your hardest.

DON'T boo your opponents, argue with the judges, complain about the results of contests, or cheat.

DO cheer and chant about your color, and sing about positive things at your camp. Say encouraging things about the other colors whenever possible.

DON'T put down other team colors in your songs or skits.

DO respect the camp property while decorating your cabin or other areas to show your team color spirit.

DON'T paint, mark, or disfigure any part of camp. This includes cabins, trees, rocks, and other camp property. Once Color Games ends, you will need to restore the camp to its original condition.

Color Games are usually planned by the camp director and camp staff. If your camp doesn't have Color Games, you may want to talk to someone in charge about starting them the following year. Bring them this book and get the ball rolling on making a rip-roaring, sports-tastic, crazy-fun Color Games happen at your camp!

CHAPTER 7

SING SING SING!

And Drive Your Counselor Crazy

Warm Up Your Voice

While most camps have their own favorites, your group might be called upon to lead a song or two, so having the words to a few classics might be helpful.

How to Sing a Camp Song!

Many camps have special camp-spirit songs that are unique to their camp, and every camp sings popular camp songs in a certain way. In fact, one of the fun debates between campers from different camps is how to sing a camp song properly. Here are some general guidelines for singing the following camp songs:

* These are fun songs, so imagine yourself singing loudly and off-key with a hundred of your friends, and don't worry too much about carrying a tune.
* Most of them are sung "chant"-style, which means they sound more like a cheer than a song.
* There is no wrong way to sing a camp song—of course, except for the way your friends from other camps sing them!

Repeat-Style Songs

These are the easiest songs to lead and learn. The song leader simply sings (or shouts) the words to the crowd, who respond with the same words.

....

"THE GREEN GRASS GROWS ALL AROUND"

There was a tree (group repeats)
All in the wood, (group repeats)
The prettiest tree (group repeats)
That you ever did see. (group repeats)

All together:

Oh, the tree in a hole,
And the hole in the ground,
And the green grass grows all around,
    all around.
The green grass grows all around.

And on that tree (group repeats)
There was a limb, (group repeats)
The prettiest limb (group repeats)
That you ever did see. (group repeats)

All together:

Oh, the limb on the tree,
And the tree in a hole,
And the hole in the ground,
And the green grass grows all around,
    all around.
The green grass grows all around.

Continue the rest of the song repeating in this style:

And on that limb
There was a branch,
The prettiest branch
That you ever did see.

Oh, the branch on the limb,
And the limb on the tree,
And the tree in a hole,
And the hole in the ground,
And the green grass grows all around,
    all around.
The green grass grows all around.

And on that branch
There was a nest,
The prettiest nest
That you ever did see.

Oh, the nest on the branch…
And the green grass grows all around,
    all around.
The green grass grows all around.

And in that nest
There was an egg,
The prettiest egg
That you ever did see.

Oh, the egg in the nest...
And the green grass grows all around,
    all around.
The green grass grows all around.

And in that egg
There was a bird,
The prettiest bird
That you ever did see.

Oh, the bird in the egg...
And the green grass grows all around,
    all around.
The green grass grows all around.

And on that bird
There was a wing,
The prettiest wing
That you ever did see.

Oh, the wing on the bird...
And the green grass grows all around,
    all around.
The green grass grows all around.

And on that wing
There was a feather,
The prettiest feather
That you ever did see.

Oh, the feather on the wing,
And the wing on the bird,
And the bird in the egg,
And the egg in the nest,
And the nest on the branch,
And the branch on the limb,
And the limb on the tree,
And the tree in a hole,
And the hole in the ground,
And the green grass grows all around,
    all around.
The green grass grows all around.
Oh, the green grass grows all around,
    all around.
The green grass grows all around!

"BOOM CHICK-A BOOM"

You should emphasize the phrase "Boom Chick-a-Boom," but really emphasize the words in **bold**!

> I said a **BOOM** Chick-a Boom *(group repeats)*
> I said a Boom **CHICK**-A Boom *(group repeats)*
> I said a Boom Chick-a Rock-a, Chick-a Rock-a, Chick-a **BOOM** *(group repeats)*
> Oh, yeah *(group repeats)*
> Uh, huh *(group repeats)*
> One more time *(group repeats)*
> (insert silly style here) style *(group repeats)*

You can make up your own styles by adding fun accents, or changing the words slightly. Here are some examples:

loud

whisper

opera-style

underwater—run your finger over your lips as you sing to make a gargling sound.

rock and roll—sing each chorus very dramatically, eyes-closed, pump your fists, you get the idea…

Camp Songs with Motions

These each have special movements to go with the songs. Use our suggestions, or be silly and make up your own!

....

"HEAD, SHOULDERS, KNEES, AND TOES"

(touch each body part as you're saying it)

Head, shoulders, knees, and toes.
    Knees and toes!
Head, shoulders, knees, and toes.
    Knees and toes!
Eyes and ears and mouth and nose.
Head, shoulders, knees, and toes.
    Knees and toes!
(hmm), shoulders, knees, and toes.
    Knees and toes!
(hmm), shoulders, knees, and toes.
    Knees and toes!
Eyes and ears and mouth and nose.
(hmm), shoulders, knees, and toes.
    Knees and toes!

Keep singing the song this way, and in each verse replace the names of a new body part with a hum, so by the end of the song, you're singing it like this:

(hmm), (hmm) (hmm), (hmm), and (hmm).
    (hmm) and (hmm)!
(hmm), (hmm) (hmm), (hmm),
    and (hmm). (hmm) and (hmm)!
(hmm) and (hmm) and (hmm)
    and (hmm).
(hmm), (hmm) (hmm), and (hmm).
    (hmm) and (hmm)!

"DO YOUR EARS HANG LOW?"

Do your ears hang low?
    (Make a motion with both hands from your ears to your shoulders, almost as if you were fanning yourself)
Do they wobble to and fro?
    (Hold your hands out in front of you, and wave your hands from side to side)
Can you tie them in a knot? *(Make a quick rolling motion with your hands)*

Can you tie them in a bow?
    (Make a quick motion with both hands, as if you were drawing a heart in the air in front of you)
Can you throw them o'er your shoulder
    (pretend you're slinging a bag over your shoulder with both hands) like a Continental soldier? *(Salute)*
Do your ears hang low?
Repeat faster and faster each time.

Classic Camp Songs

"THE ANTS GO MARCHING"

The ants go marching one by one,
  hurrah, hurrah!
The ants go marching one by one,
  hurrah, hurrah!
The ants go marching one by one,
The little one stops to suck his thumb.
And they all go marching down into
  the ground
To get out of the rain. BOOM! BOOM!
  BOOM!

The ants go marching two by two,
  hurrah, hurrah!
The ants go marching two by two,
  hurrah, hurrah!
The ants go marching two by two,
The little one stops to tie his shoe.
And they all go marching down into
  the ground
To get out of the rain. BOOM!
  BOOM! BOOM!

The ants go marching three by three,
  hurrah, hurrah!
The ants go marching three by three,
  hurrah, hurrah!
The ants go marching three by three,

The little one stops to climb a tree.
And they all go marching down into
  the ground
To get out of the rain. BOOM!
  BOOM! BOOM!

The ants go marching four by four,
  hurrah, hurrah!
The ants go marching four by four,
  hurrah, hurrah!
The ants go marching four by four,
The little one stops to shut the door.
And they all go marching down into
  the ground
To get out of the rain. BOOM!
  BOOM! BOOM!

The ants go marching five by five,
  hurrah, hurrah!
The ants go marching five by five,
  hurrah, hurrah!
The ants go marching five by five,
The little one stops to take a dive.
And they all go marching down into
  the ground
To get out of the rain. BOOM!
  BOOM! BOOM!

The ants go marching six by six,
    hurrah, hurrah!
The ants go marching six by six,
    hurrah, hurrah!
The ants go marching six by six,
The little one stops to pick up sticks.
And they all go marching down into
    the ground
To get out of the rain. BOOM!
    BOOM! BOOM!

The ants go marching seven by seven,
    hurrah, hurrah!
The ants go marching seven by seven,
    hurrah, hurrah!
The ants go marching seven by seven,
The little one stops to pray to heaven.
And they all go marching down into
    the ground
To get out of the rain. BOOM!
    BOOM! BOOM!

The ants go marching eight by eight,
    hurrah, hurrah!
The ants go marching eight by eight,
    hurrah, hurrah!
The ants go marching eight by eight,

The little one stops to shut the gate.
And they all go marching down into
    the ground
To get out of the rain. BOOM!
    BOOM! BOOM!

The ants go marching nine by nine,
    hurrah, hurrah!
The ants go marching nine by nine,
    hurrah, hurrah!
The ants go marching nine by nine,
The little one stops to check the time.
And they all go marching down into
    the ground
To get out of the rain. BOOM!
    BOOM! BOOM!

The ants go marching ten by ten,
    hurrah, hurrah!
The ants go marching ten by ten,
    hurrah, hurrah!
The ants go marching ten by ten,
The little one stops to say "THE END."
And they all go marching down into
    the ground
To get out of the rain. BOOM!
    BOOM! BOOM!

"JOHN JACOB JINGLEHEIMER SCHMIDT"

John Jacob Jingleheimer Schmidt,
His name is my name, too!
Whenever we go out
The people always shout
"There goes John Jacob Jingleheimer
    Schmidt!"
Na-na-na-na-na-na-na!
(Repeat)

Each time you repeat the song, it should get quieter and quieter, except "Na-na-na-na-na-na-na!" which you should sing as loudly as you can.

"ON TOP OF OLD SMOKEY"

(If you feel like being really silly, you can always substitute these words with the lyrics to "On Top of Spaghetti.")

On top of Old Smokey
All covered with snow,
I lost my true lover
For a'courtin' too slow.

Now courtin's a pleasure
And partin's a grief,
But a false-hearted lover
Is worse than a thief.

'Cause a thief he will rob you
And take what you have,
But a false-hearted lover
Will take you to your grave.

And the grave will decay you
And turn you to dust,
But where is the young man
That a poor girl can trust.

They'll hug you and kiss you
And tell you more lies
Than the crossties on railroads
Or the stars in the sky.

They'll tell you they love you
To give your heart ease,
But the moment your back's turned,
They'll court whom they please.

Bury me on Old Smokey,
Old Smokey so high,
So the wild birds in heaven
Will hear my sad cry.

On top of Old Smokey
All covered with snow,
I lost my true lover
For a'courtin' too slow.

"SHE'LL BE COMING 'ROUND THE MOUNTAIN"

She'll be coming 'round the mountain
   when she comes.
She'll be coming 'round the mountain
   when she comes.
She'll be coming 'round the mountain,
   she'll be coming 'round the
   mountain,
She'll be coming 'round the mountain
   when she comes.

She'll be driving six white horses when
   she comes.
She'll be driving six white horses when
   she comes.
She'll be driving six white horses, she'll
   be driving six white horses,
She'll be driving six white horses when
   she comes.

Oh, we'll all go out to meet her when
   she comes.
Oh, we'll all go out to meet her when
   she comes.

Oh, we'll all go out to meet her, we'll all
   go out to meet her,
We'll all go out to meet her when she
   comes.

She'll be wearing red pajamas when
   she comes.
She'll be wearing red pajamas when
   she comes.
She'll be wearing red pajamas, she'll be
   wearing red pajamas,
She'll be wearing red pajamas when
   she comes.

She will have to sleep with Grandma
   when she comes.
She will have to sleep with Grandma
   when she comes.
She will have to sleep with Grandma,
   she will have to sleep with Grandma,
She will have to sleep with Grandma
   when she comes.

CHAPTER 8

AWESOME ARTS AND COOL CRAFTS
Be a Crafty Kid!

Get Creative on Your Own

Between scheduled activities at camp, there are lots of ways to spend your time creatively. We recommend these crafts because they are easy to complete, fun to create, make great gifts, and can be done while hanging out with your friends. Your camp might even give you an opportunity to do these crafts during regularly scheduled activity time.

Friendship Bracelets

Making friends is the most important part of camp, right? Well, making friendship bracelets may become one of your favorite activities. All you need to make the bracelets are a few different colors of embroidery floss and a few friends to give the bracelets to!

Your camp might have some embroidery thread in the craft supply closet for you to use. You also might want to purchase some extra at a craft store before you go to camp to be sure you have enough to last you the whole summer or to share with your friends. Your friends might have brought enough for you to share, which is the true meaning of making friendship bracelets.

THE BASIC FRIENDSHIP BRACELET

This bracelet is the easiest to make and looks really cool.

1. To start, select three different-color strings, and cut each about three feet long (approximately the length from your shoulder to your wrist).

2. Tie all the strings together with a simple knot, leaving about three inches of "tail" on the end.

3. Attach the string to a book or table using masking tape, or use your counselor's clipboard. This keeps the strings in place as you pull on them to weave the bracelet.

4. Take one string and wrap it around the other strings. Make a basic knot over the two remaining strings and pull tight.

5. Repeat this step with the same colored string ten times, or until you have a 1/4-inch band of one color.

6. Once you complete the first band, repeat steps 4 and 5, using a different-color string. Repeat steps 4 and 5 with your third color.

7. Once you've used each string once as the "outside" color, repeat the pattern until the bracelet is long enough to go around a wrist, ankle, or neck. You can modify the number of strings, color-band sizes, and color patterns however you want. Be creative!

8. When you're finished, tie another knot at the end of the bracelet using all of the strings, and leave about three inches of "tail."

9. Tie the friendship bracelet around your friend's wrist.

THE FLAT STRIPED FRIENDSHIP BRACELET

This bracelet looks more fancy but it's not much harder to make.

1. Follow steps 1 to 3 in the Basic Friendship Bracelet instructions. For a thicker bracelet, use at least four different colored strings.

2. Decide which order you would like your color bands to appear, and line up your strings in that way.

3. Moving left to right, wrap the first string around the string directly next to it and make a simple knot. Do this step twice. Then go to the next string in line and wrap and knot the first string over that one twice. Continue until you've wrapped and knotted the first string with every string in the line. This will create your first band of color.

4. Take your second string and repeat step 2. Be sure to go in the same order, left to right.

5. Take your third string and repeat step 2 in the correct color order.

6. Take your fourth string and repeat step 2 in the correct color order.

7. Keep cycling through your colors in this way creating a stripe pattern until the bracelet fits around your wrist or ankle.

8. Follow steps 8 to 10 of the Basic Friendship Bracelet instructions to finish your bracelet.

Here's an example using colored strings in the following order: Red, White, Blue, and Yellow. Here's how you make the color bands:

BAND 1: Red over White x 2
Red over Blue x 2
Red over Yellow x 2

BAND 2: White over Red x 2
White over Blue x 2
White over Yellow x 2

BAND 3: Blue over Red x 2
Blue over White x 2
Blue over Yellow x 2

BAND 4: Yellow over Red x 2
Yellow over White x 2
Yellow over Blue x 2

MAKE YOUR OWN STRIPED FRIENDSHIP BRACELET DESIGNS

Once you've made the basic striped friendship bracelet, it's easy and fun to make your own designs. The basic design above uses two wraps for every string. If you want to try something different, you can create thick bands of one color separated by a thin band of another, simply by using more strings of one color (i.e. four blue strings) and fewer strings of another color (i.e. two white strings) to make your bracelet.

Or, you can try this fancy design:

THE "V"-STRIPED BRACELET

This is a very cool bracelet. To make one, just follow these simple steps.

1. Choose four different colors of string that you like and cut two three-foot lengths of each color.

2. Decide which order you would like the bands of color to appear, and lay out in that order from left to right the first four colored strings. Say you chose red, white, blue, and yellow; your first four strings would be lined up in that order.

3. Lay the next four strings in the opposite order so that they reflect the first four strings like a mirror image. Your strings from left to right would be red, white, blue, yellow, yellow, blue, white, and red.

4. Tie the strings together by making a simple knot about 2 inches from the top of all of the strings. Keep the strings in the proper order and separate them into a left side and a right side—this will help you keep them from getting mixed up.

5. For the left-side strings only, moving from left to right wrap the first string around the string directly next to it and make a simple knot. Do this step twice. Then go to the next string in color order, and wrap and knot the first string twice over it. Continue doing this, until you've wrapped and knotted the first string with every other string on the left side.

6. Repeat the step above with the right-side strings, but do it from right to left. Starting with the string all the way on the right side, wrap and knot it around the string directly to the left of it. Do this step twice. Then go to the next string in color order, and wrap and knot the first string twice over it. Continue doing this, until you've wrapped and knotted the first string with every other string on the right side.

7. Once you've completed steps 5 and 6 with the first color, join the two sides and create the "V"-shape. To do this, wrap the right-side first string around the left-side first string, both of which should now be in the middle, and tie them in a knot.

8. Now you're ready to start steps 5 and 6 all over again with the next color in your order. Continue steps 5, 6, and 7 until your bracelet is long enough, then tie a large knot with all the strings to finish it.

Tie Dye

I t just wouldn't be summer camp without making a tie-dye T-shirt. These shirts are bright and colorful, and will remind you of camp well after the summer ends. Chances are your camp will give you an opportunity to make tie-dye shirts, so use these tips to make some cool patterns.

Tips to tie dye by...

* Wear rubber gloves to keep your hands from turning different colors from the dye.
* Wear old clothes, or ones that you can ruin, when you tie-dye, because if dye gets on them it's staying on them!
* Be sure to let your tie-dyed article completely dry before you wear it.
* The first time you wash the article, put it in the washer by itself so that dye does not rub off onto your other clothes.
* Be careful not to get the dye in your mouth or eyes. If you do, rinse immediately and tell a counselor.

A Quick Overview

1. Grab a clean, white shirt and bundle it up. You can roll the shirt, twist it, or bunch it into a tight ball.

2. Wrap rubber bands or string in different patterns around the bundled shirt.

3. Dip the sections (separated by the rubber bands or string you've tied around it) of the shirt into different colored dyes. For example, you could dip one half of your white shirt into a yellow dye, and then hold the shirt by the newly dyed yellow side and dip the remaining white half into a blue dye. You can dye your shirt with as many colors as you like!

4. When you take the rubber bands or rope off your shirt, you will have created very cool and unique designs.

Tips and Tricks for Great Tie-Dye

* **Recycle old, white T-shirts and pillow cases,** even those that have writing or pictures on them. Tie-dye is a great way to give your dingy old T-shirt some new life, plus it will make that old ketchup stain look like part of a great design! Be sure only to tie-dye items that you have permission from your parents to use.

* **Thoroughly soak your shirt in clean water before you begin to fold** and put rubber bands on it. This makes the shirt easier to fold and band tightly, which keeps the colors from running together. Squeeze out the excess water before you start dyeing.

* **Wrap the rubber bands around the shirt as tightly as you can.** Twist the rubber band around the shirt in the same spot as many times as possible to make it tight. Wrapping the rubber bands tightly helps keep the colors from running together, and creates very cool web patterns when you untie it.

* **Hold the shirt in the dye for several minutes.** If you dip your shirt in the dye for only ten to fifteen seconds, it may look bright when you first unroll it, but the color will fade quickly. Hold the shirt, or a particular section, in the dye for several minutes at a time. If you get bored waiting, why don't you make up a song about tie-dyeing?

* **Don't "double-dip."** Try to dip only white parts of your shirt into different vats of dye. If you dip a freshly dyed red shirt section into blue dye, you may love the color it makes on your shirt, but everyone who dips after you will get purple instead of blue.

SPIRAL TYE-DYE

1. Thoroughly soak your T-shirt in clean water. Squeeze out the excess water.

2. Lay it flat on the ground or table.

3. Pinch the shirt in the middle with your thumb and forefinger and twist your fingers. Be sure that you pinch both the front and back side of the shirt. You will see the shirt start to make spiral folds.

4. Continue to twist the shirt until the whole thing is folded in a spiral pattern.

5. Squeeze the shirt together keeping it flat, and wrap several rubber bands tightly across the spiral so that the bands divide the shirt into three or four pie-shaped sections.

6. Dip each different pie-shaped section of the shirt into different colored dyes. Be careful to only put one section of the shirt into one dye bucket.

7. Take off the rubber bands, unwind the shirt, and admire!

BULLS-EYE TIE-DYE

1. Thoroughly soak your T-shirt in clean water. Squeeze out the excess water.

2. Lay it flat on the ground or table.

3. Pinch the shirt in the middle and lift the shirt up from the table. Be sure that your pinch caught both the front and back of your shirt.

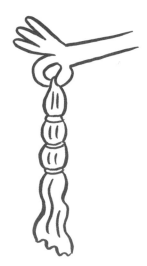

4. Twist the shirt into a tight tube, keeping the pinched part in your hands.

5. Wrap rubber bands tightly around the pinched part of your shirt, about one inch from your fingertips. This part of the shirt is the "tip."

6. Wrap more rubber bands tightly three inches below the tip. Continue wrapping rubber bands every three inches until you get to the end of the shirt. Your shirt should look like a tube at this point, and you should have three or four rubber bands wrapping around your shirt.

7. Dip the tip of the shirt up to the first rubber band into one color of dye for several minutes.

8. Dip the end of the shirt opposite the tip into the dye up to the rubber band for several minutes.

9. Fold the shirt in half between the remaining white sections and dip this into another color for several minutes, taking care not to dip the already dyed sections into this new color.

10. Fold that same section of shirt in half in the opposite direction so that you can thoroughly dye the other side of that band.

11. Take off the rubber bands and unwind the shirt. Once your shirt is dry, wear your tie-dye with pride!

THREE-STRIPE DESIGN

1. Thoroughly soak your T-shirt in clean water. Squeeze out the excess water.

2. Lie the shirt flat, with the neck facing up. Pretend like it's a rolling pin and roll the shirt into a tube.

3. Divide the shirt into three sections by wrapping two rubber bands around the middle of the shirt several inches apart from each other. The sections don't need to be even—in fact, uneven sections add special flair.

4. Dip the first section into one color of dye for several minutes. Wring out the excess dye when you remove it.

5. Dip the bottom section into a different color, like you did in instruction #4.

6. Fold the shirt in half in the middle of the remaining white section and dip this into another color for several minutes, taking care not to dip the already dyed sections into this new color.

7. Fold that same section of shirt in half in the opposite direction so that you can thoroughly dye the other side.

8. When you take off the rubber bands and unravel the shirt you will have a triple-striped shirt that looks very cool!

100

BLOTTED PATTERN

This one uses dyes, but no ties.

* Thoroughly soak your T-shirt in clean water. Squeeze out the excess water.

* Lay your shirt out flat on the ground or table.

* Pour different dyes into cups, spray bottles, or empty ketchup/mustard bottles.

* Squirt or pour small amounts of dye onto the shirt in random patterns until you see a design you like.

CHAPTER 9

CAMPFIRE STORIES AND FUNNY SKITS

More Excuses to Act Silly

How Entertaining!

What really makes summer camp unique is the tradition of performing around campfires or during assembly time, when the entire camp gets together to have some fun. Skits and campfire stories have been part of summer camp for many years.

Stories have been told around the campfire for as long as there have been campfires. Sometimes the stories are funny, sometimes they are scary, and sometimes they have a lesson to be learned. Other stories may tell the legends of your camp, including things that happened in the past or how the camp got its name.

Campfire Stories

Here are a few stories you may want to share one night around the campfire.

....

"HOW BEAR LOST HIS TAIL"
(a Native American Folktale)

A long time ago, Bear had a long, black tail that he loved to show off. He would walk around the forest wagging his tail so that everyone could see it. Fox would watch Bear as he walked around the forest and after a while grew tired of seeing him show off. One day, Fox decided he was going to play a trick on Bear.

It was wintertime, and everything was covered in snow and ice. Even the lake was frozen. Fox made a hole in the ice and, being very clever, was able to catch some fish and place them on the ice near the hole. When Bear walked by, wagging his tail as usual, he saw that Fox had caught a great many fish.

"Hello, Fox, what are you doing?" said Bear.

"Hello, Bear, I was hungry and decided to do some fishing. Would you like to give it a try?" answered Fox.

"Oh yes, I love fish!" cried Bear.

Fox motioned for Bear to walk over onto the ice where the hole was and explained to Bear how he had been so lucky at catching fish.

"First," said Fox, "you must sit with your tail in the water. When a fish bites it, you pull up your tail as fast as you can."

"If I cannot see the water, how will I know that a fish is biting my tail?" said Bear.

"I'll hide behind the trees over there where the fish cannot see me, and when one bites your tail, I will shout. But it is very important that you do not move until I tell you to."

"I will do it." said Bear.

Bear sat down by the hole in the ice and put his long, beautiful tail in the water. Fox watched him for a while, to be sure Bear was following all of his instructions. Then he snuck off to go home. The next morning, Fox woke up and thought about Bear.

"I wonder if he is still there," said Fox.

Fox made his way back to the lake and saw Bear sitting on the ice, fast asleep with his tail in the water. It had been so cold during the night that the hole had frozen around Bear's tail. Fox quietly crept up to Bear and shouted "Now, Bear!"

Bear woke up with a start and pulled his tail as hard as he could, hoping that he had caught a fish. Instead, his tail broke off and stayed in the ice. And that's how Bear lost his tail.

"THE UNLUCKY MAN"
(Based on an Afghani Folktale)

Once there was a man who lived in a beautiful log cabin. He seemed to have everything, but was never happy. The man believed it was because he was unlucky.

One day he had enough, and he went to a very old and wise woman to find out why he was not lucky. The old and wise woman thought about it and told him he must visit The Old Man of the Mountain and ask him that question.

"Where do I find The Old Man of the Mountain?" the man asked.

"Travel west until you reach the end of the world, and there you will find The Old Man of the Mountain," said the old woman.

So the man set off to find The Old Man of the Mountain to ask why he was not lucky. He walked for a day, he walked for a week, he walked for a month, and he even walked for a year, until he came to a clearing, which was surrounded by wolves. On one side there were strong and vicious-looking wolves. On the other side was a small, scrawny wolf. The man decided to walk toward the scrawny wolf.

The wolf asked, "Where are you going?"

"I am going to visit The Old Man of the Mountain to ask him why I have no luck," answered the man.

"Interesting. If you find him, can you please ask why I am not as strong and as vicious as my brothers?" asked the wolf.

"Of course," the man answered as he walked off.

The man walked for a day, he walked for a week, he walked for a month, and he walked for a year, until he arrived at a beautiful forest. The trees were vast and stretched far up into the sky, but in a small clearing was a short, leafless tree with wimpy branches. As the man walked by, the tree called out, "Excuse me, where are you going?"

"I am going to visit The Old Man of the Mountain to ask him why I have no luck."

"Fascinating. If you find The Old Man of the Mountain, can you ask him why I am not as tall and strong as my brothers?" the tree asked.

"Of course," answered the man as he continued walking.

The man walked for a day, he walked for a week, he walked for a month, and he walked for a year, until he came to a small, blue house. Surrounding this house was a beautiful garden filled with vibrant colors and bright flowers. Inside the house was the most beautiful woman the man had ever seen. On seeing the man, the woman invited him in for dinner. The man agreed and enjoyed a wonderful feast cooked to perfection by the woman. As they ate the man told his story.

At the end of his story the woman said, "That is a lovely story. If you find The Old Man of the Mountain, can you ask him why I am so lonely?"

"Of course I can," answered the man.

The next day, the man set off and walked west. He walked for a day, he walked for a week, he walked for a month, and he walked for a year, until finally he reached the end of the world. There, sitting on a rock, fishing, was The Old Man of the Mountain.

The man called out, "Excuse me, Old Man of the Mountain. Can you tell me why I have no luck?"

The Old Man of the Mountain looked up and said, "You have all the luck you need. It is all around you, but you don't notice it. Be more observant and you will find your luck."

This made sense to the man. He began to ask the questions he had promised the others he'd ask, but The Old Man of the Mountain raised his hand.

"There is no need to ask your questions. I already know what they are, for I know everything." And with that, the Old Man of the Mountain whispered the answers into the man's ear. The man thanked him and began to walk home. He arrived first at the beautiful woman's house and knocked on the door. The woman was overjoyed to see him and asked for her answer.

"The Old Man of the Mountain told me that you must get married if you want to cure your lonliness."

"Of course! That makes sense. Will you marry me?" the woman asked the man.

"I am sorry. I cannot, for I must find my luck. But the first nice man I see, I will send him back to you," answered the man.

With that he continued home, until he reached the beautiful forest. The small tree saw him and asked for his answer.

"The Old Man of the Mountain told me the reason you are small and have no leaves is because buried beneath your roots is a chest full of gold. It is blocking you from receiving nutrients."

"Of course! That makes sense. Some workmen left shovels over there. If you dig up the chest, you can keep the gold inside," said the tree.

"I am sorry. I cannot, for I must find my luck. But the first strong man I see, I will send him back," replied the man. And with that, he continued on his way home.

The man reached the clearing of the wolves, and the small, scrawny wolf asked him for his answer.

"The Old Man of the Mountain told me the reason you are small and scrawny is because you do not eat enough. You must eat the first big, stupid animal you see."

And the wolf did.

"ONCE BITTEN"
(Tell this story in a spooky way)

One summer, I went to a traveling carnival. My friend and I spent the day riding on all the rides and having a good time. We came upon a fortune-teller booth and thought it would be fun to have our palms read. My friend went first and was told that he was going to lead a healthy, happy life.

When it came time for my turn, the fortune teller took my palm and looked at me very strangely. She asked me if I was fond of dogs, and I told her, "Yes." She said that in a previous life I had been a dog, but I had been treated poorly by my owner, who kept me tied up with a heavy chain. She told me that one time I tried so hard to escape the chain that it broke my collarbone. In fact, my collarbone still has a knot in it from this experience. Go ahead and feel right here... BARK!

(Encourage the person next to you to feel your collarbone, and when he does, bark loudly and pretend like you're going to bite his hand.)

Skits

Skits are short plays that usually end up being funny or silly at the end. They can be performed at any time during the day, though campfires and assembly times tend to be the best because you have a captive audience. Have lots of fun with these, and remember to speak loud enough for everyone to hear you!

"IS IT TIME YET?"

Five or more people sit on a bench, each with their right leg crossed over their left. The person at the end of the bench says to the person beside him "Is it time yet?"

The second person on the bench then says the same thing to the person next to him, who then says it to the person next to him, and so on, until the message gets to the last person on the bench.

The last person on the bench checks his watch and says "No," to the person beside him. Then that person relays the message back to the next person, and so on, until it gets back to the first person on the bench.

Then the first person on the bench launches into the same routine again, asking "Is it time yet?" and sending the message down the line of people on the bench. Repeat the routine twice more, with each person getting more impatient each time. The third time the message gets passed along, the last person on the bench should answer "Yes."

Then everyone crosses their left leg over their right leg.

BUBBLE GUM

You will need four campers and a chair. The gum is imaginary.

Set up the chair in the middle of what you designate as your stage.

The first camper walks out to the chair, chewing gum in a dramatic fashion. She takes the gum out of her mouth, places it on the back of the chair, then walks off stage.

The second camper walks out to the chair, leans on the back of it, and finds the gum on his hand. Acting totally disgusted, he wipes it on the seat of the chair and walks off.

The third camper walks out to the chair and sits down. She realizes with great disgust that the gum is stuck to her bottom. Acting disgusted, she peels it off, throws it to the ground, and walks off.

The fourth camper walks out to the chair, but realizes he's got gum stuck to his shoe. Acting annoyed, he peels it off, sticks it to the back of the chair, and walks off.

Then the first camper comes back onto the stage, walks up to the chair, peels it off, happily sticks it in her mouth, and walks off.

WEE!!!

Three campers lay on the ground, side-by-side, and pretend to be asleep. The fourth camper, who is acting as the camp counselor, tells the campers that it's time for bed and then lies down side-by-side with the group.

The camper lying the farthest away from the counselor crawls around the back of the other campers and asks the counselor if he can go wee.

The counselor says "No! Now go back to sleep." The camper crawls back to his spot. He lets a few seconds pass, then crawls over again and tells the counselor "I really got to go wee!"

The counselor replies, "*No,* go back to sleep now!"

The camper then crawls back behind the other campers. Once more, he crawls back and says to the counselor, "I really reallly reeeallllly got to go wee!"

The counselor says "Well, if you have to go that bad…go ahead."

The camper gleefully gets up and skips around yelling, "*WEE, WEE, WEE!!!*"

IS IT TIME FOR JAPUTCHA?

A counselor, or a camper who is playing the counselor, sits in the middle of the stage. The additional campers begin trotting around the counselor in a circle, making whooping sounds. After the campers complete one circle around the counselor, begin the skit.

Camper 1: Excuse me, Counselor, but is it time for Japutcha?

Counselor: I will ask. Oh, Spirit of the Mountain, is it time for Japutcha? *(Counselor pauses for three seconds)* No.

(Campers run another circle around the Counselor, whooping and hollering)

Camper 2: Excuse me, Counselor, is it time for Japutcha?

Counselor: I will ask. Oh, Spirit of the Lake, is it time for Japutcha? *(Counselor pauses for three seconds)* No.

(Campers run another circle around the Counselor, and the hollering gets more wild and animated)

Camper 3: Excuse me, Counselor, is it time for Japutcha?

Counselor: I will ask. Oh, Spirit of the Sky, is it time for Japutcha? *(Counselor pauses for three seconds)* No.

(Campers run another circle around the Counselor—the noises and motions of the group are getting stranger and sillier)

Camper 4: Excuse me, Counselor, is it time for Japutcha?

Counselor: I will ask. Oh, Spirit of the Wind, is it time for Japutcha? *(Counselor pauses for three seconds)* No.

(Campers run another circle around the Counselor, this time the silliest and weirdest of all)

Camper 5: Excuse me, Counselor, is it time for Japutcha?

Counselor: I will ask. Great Spirits of the Mountain, Lake, Sky, and Wind, is it time for Japutcha? *(Counselor pauses for three seconds)* The spirits have spoken, and they have said that it is time for Japutcha. You may begin.

(All campers in the circle turn to face the Counselor)

All: Japutcha right hand in, Japutcha right hand out, Japutcha right hand in, and Ja shake it all about... *(campers perform the "Hokey-Pokey")*

IMPORTANT PAPERS

You will need two campers for this skit. You will also need various pieces of paper in different sizes and colors, and a roll of toilet paper. One camper will be Important Person—he could act like a king, a president, or a businessman. The other person plays Assistant.

Important Person: Oh, Assistant, would you bring me my important papers?

(Assistant runs toward Important Person with some sheets of paper)

Assistant: Are these your important papers?

Important Person: No. Please, you must get me my important papers.

(Assistant runs toward Important Person with some different papers)

Assistant: Are these your important papers?

Important Person: No. Please, you must hurry. Get me my important papers.

(Assistant runs toward Important Person with some different papers)

Assistant: Are these your important papers?

Important Person *(very impatient and jumping around)*: No, no, no! You must get me my important papers NOW!

(Assistant runs toward Important Person with a roll of toilet paper)

Assistant: Are THESE your important papers?

Important Person: Ah yes, my important papers. Thank you, Assistant.

(The Important Person runs off the stage, relieved)

CHAPTER 10

THE LAST DAY

It's Not "Goodbye," It's "Talk to You Soon!"

Keep your camp friends and camp memories

The last day of camp is sometimes harder than the first day of camp. It is difficult to say goodbye to friends you've made and good times you've had. After spending so much time at camp, it may be hard to think about what a day without camp might be like. When the time comes to say goodbye, know this: your time at camp, whether it was two weeks or two months, will give you memories that will last a lifetime.

You will have shared great moments with wonderful people, and those are the things you will remember. And just because you will be leaving camp doesn't mean that you can't keep in touch with your camp friends. There are many different ways to stay connected to everyone: e-mail, instant messenger, phone calls, or good old-fashioned letter writing.

Use this section to stay in touch with your new best friends and help make your camp memories last. There are spaces for multiple years, so you can bring this guidebook with you to camp next summer, and the next summer, and the summer after that....

All About My Group

Camp Name: _____ Year: _____

Bunk Name/Counselor's Name: _____

My group mates: _____

_____

_____

Camp Name: _____ Year: _____

Bunk Name/Counselor's Name: _____

My group mates: _____

_____

_____

Camp Name: _____ Year: _____

Bunk Name/Counselor's Name: _____

My group mates: _____

_____

_____

Camp Name: _____ Year: _____

Bunk Name/Counselor's Name: _____

My group mates: _____

_____

_____

My Summer Camp Memories

The funniest thing that happened at camp was…

_____

_____

The weirdest thing that happened at camp was…

_____

_____

My favorite activity was…

_____

My least-favorite activity was…

_____

My best friends from camp are…

_____

_____

The best meal was…

_____

The worst meal was…

_____

My favorite camp song is…

_____

The best game at camp is…

_____

Things I learned at camp…

_____

_____

Things I tried for the first time…

_____

_____

Bunk Diagram

(Draw a floor plan of what your bunk looked like, and who slept where.)

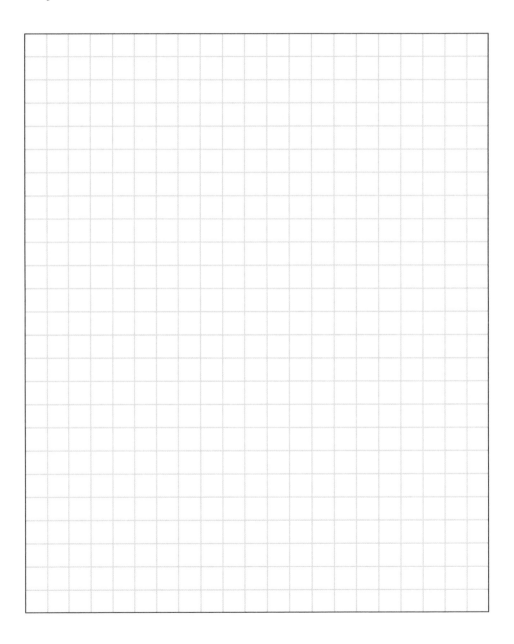

Summer Camp Reading List

If you're sad about leaving summer camp to begin the new school year, perk up! You can always *read* about summer camp adventures. Here are some classic titles that will keep you in the summer camp mood, all year long:

Baer, Judy. *Camp Pinetree Pals.* Plain City, Ohio: Darby Creek Publishing, 1991.

Belton, Sandra. *Summer Camp, Ready or Not!* New York: Simon & Schuster Children's Publishing, 1997.

Dadey, Debbie, and Marcia T. Jones. *Werewolves Don't Go to Summer Camp (The Adventures of the Bailey School Kids, #2).* New York: Scholastic, Inc., 1991.

Danziger, Paula *Hail, Hail Camp Timberwood.* New York: Pocket Books, 1980.

Fiedler, Lisa. *The Case of the Cheerleading Camp Mystery (New Adventures of Mary-Kate and Ashley No. 17).* New York: Parachute Press, 2000.

Klise, Kate. Illustrated by Sarah M. Klise *Letters from Camp.* New York: HarperTrophy, 2000.

Morgan, Melissa J. *Jenna's Dilemma (Camp Confidential).* New York: Penguin Young Readers Group, 2005.

O'Dell, Kathleen. *Agnes Parker...Happy Camper?* New York: Dial, 2005

Park, Barbara. *Buddies.* New York: Avon Books, 1986.

Paulsen, Gary. Illustrated by Ruth Paulsen. *Canoe Days.* Albuquerque, New Mexico: Dragonfly Books, 2001.

Smith, Jane Denitz. *Mary by Myself.* New York: HarperTrophy, 1999.

Spinelli, Jerry. *Dump Days.* New York: Yearling, 1991.

Stine, R. L. *Camp Nowhere (Nightmare Room No. 9).* New York: Avon Books, 2001.

Stolz, Mary. *A Wonderful, Terrible Time.* New York: Harper & Row, 1967.

Van Leeuwen, Jean. *The Great Summer Camp Catastrophe.* New York: Dial, 1992.

Warner, Gertrude Chandler, and Albert Whitman. *The Summer Camp Mystery (The Boxcar Children Mysteries, No. 82).* Morton Grove, Illinois: Albert Whitman & Company, 2001.

A Taste of Summer Camp

Sometimes the best memories are of things we've had to eat or drink. At camp, some of these memories can be either good or bad, like the awesome ice-cream sundaes you made from scratch or the gross sandwich that spoiled in the sun. Just because camp has to end doesn't mean that you can't enjoy some of those tasty summer camp treats. Check out these classic camp recipes that you can re-create at home.

BUG JUICE (a camp favorite)

First, take 1/4 pound of grasshoppers, 1/2 a cup of crickets...just kidding! Many camps have their own versions of bug juice, but it most often comes down to this: it's sweet, it's fruity, and it does *not* contain any real bugs. Fruit punch is a favorite flavor, but any flavor or color will do. The sweeter the better!

INGREDIENTS

Powdered punch

Water; look on the punch label for the correct amount.

Sugar; only add sugar if the directions on the punch mix call for it. If they do, then add until you get the taste you want.

Gummy Bugs; to give it a real buggy look!

The type of powdered punch mix you are using will really determine how you make your bug juice. You can follow all of the given directions or (with an adult's help) add some of your own ingredients to make an original concoction. Have fun!

S'MORES

If you like graham crackers, marshmallows, and chocolate, you will love S'mores. You'll feel like you're still sitting 'round the campfire!

INGREDIENTS

One stick; choose one that's a few feet long and somewhat straight, and break off the extra branches.

Chocolate squares; chocolate candy bars work the best, use one square per S'more.

Graham crackers; split one cracker in half for each S'more.

Marshmallows; use one toasted marshmallow per S'more.

1. Soak the stick with water (this keeps it from catching on fire). Put a marshmallow on the end of the stick.

2. **HAVE AN ADULT HELP YOU WITH THIS STEP**, since there is fire involved. Hold the non-marshmallow end of the stick with your hand and place your marshmallow over the fire (this can be done on a stove top if you don't have a real camp fire). Try to avoid putting your marshmallow in the fire because it will burn. If your marshmallow does catch fire, gently blow on it to put the fire out. Do not shake it because it may fly off of your stick and burn you or someone else.

3. When your marshmallow is a nice golden brown, carefully remove it from the end of the stick by pressing it between two pieces of graham cracker and pulling it off.

4. Add a piece of chocolate to the center of the graham cracker and marshmallow sandwich, and let it melt for a minute or two.

5. Enjoy your chocolaty, gooey treat!

Microwave S'mores

CAUTION: DO NOT TRY THIS ON YOUR OWN. ASK AN ADULT TO HELP YOU.

Take two graham cracker pieces, and place one marshmallow and one square of chocolate between the two crackers. Put the uncooked S'more on a microwave-safe dish, and set the timer for about 15 seconds. Be careful when you take it out of the microwave because it may be very hot.

ICE CREAM (from Scratch!)

Ask an adult for help with the measurements.

INGREDIENTS

1 tbsp. sugar

$1/2$ cup whole milk

Less than 1 tsp. vanilla extract

5 to 6 tbsp. rock salt

1 small zipper-seal plastic bag

1 large zipper-seal plastic bag

Ice cubes (enough to fill the large bag halfway)

Put the sugar, milk, and vanilla in the small bag, and seal it closed. Fill the big bag halfway with ice and rock salt. Put the small bag inside the big bag and seal the big bag. Shake the bags for a few minutes or until you see the mixture becoming solid.

You've made ice cream!

Autographs

Have your friends autograph these pages so you
can remember them always...

Autographs

Autographs

Autographs

Autographs

Addresses

Stay in touch!

Name	**Name**
Address	Address
City, State, and Zip Code	**City, State, and Zip Code**
Phone	Phone
E-mail	**E-mail**
What I will remember most about this person…	**What I will remember most about this person…**
Name	Name
Address	Address
City, State, and Zip Code	City, State, and Zip Code
Phone	Phone
E-mail	E-mail
What I will remember most about this person…	What I will remember most about this person…
Name	**Name**
Address	Address
City, State, and Zip Code	**City, State, and Zip Code**
Phone	**Phone**
E-mail	**E-mail**
What I will remember most about this person…	**What I will remember most about this person…**

Name	Name
Address	Address
City, State, and Zip Code	City, State, and Zip Code
Phone	Phone
E-mail	E-mail
What I will remember most about this person…	What I will remember most about this person…
Name	**Name**
Address	**Address**
City, State, and Zip Code	**City, State, and Zip Code**
Phone	**Phone**
E-mail	**E-mail**
What I will remember most about this person…	**What I will remember most about this person…**
Name	Name
Address	Address
City, State, and Zip Code	City, State, and Zip Code
Phone	Phone
E-mail	E-mail
What I will remember most about this person…	What I will remember most about this person…
Name	**Name**
Address	**Address**
City, State, and Zip Code	**City, State, and Zip Code**
Phone	**Phone**
E-mail	**E-mail**
What I will remember most about this person…	**What I will remember most about this person…**

Name

Address

City, State, and Zip Code

Phone

E-mail

What I will remember most about this person...

Name

Address

City, State, and Zip Code

Phone

E-mail

What I will remember most about this person...

Name

Address

City, State, and Zip Code

Phone

E-mail

What I will remember most about this person...

Name

Address

City, State, and Zip Code

Phone

E-mail

What I will remember most about this person...

Name

Address

City, State, and Zip Code

Phone

E-mail

What I will remember most about this person...

Name

Address

City, State, and Zip Code

Phone

E-mail

What I will remember most about this person...

Name

Address

City, State, and Zip Code

Phone

E-mail

What I will remember most about this person...

Name

Address

City, State, and Zip Code

Phone

E-mail

What I will remember most about this person...

Name

Address

City, State, and Zip Code

Phone

E-mail

What I will remember most about this person…

Name

Address

City, State, and Zip Code

Phone

E-mail

What I will remember most about this person…

Name

Address

City, State, and Zip Code

Phone

E-mail

What I will remember most about this person…

Name

Address

City, State, and Zip Code

Phone

E-mail

What I will remember most about this person…

Name

Address

City, State, and Zip Code

Phone

E-mail

What I will remember most about this person…

Name

Address

City, State, and Zip Code

Phone

E-mail

What I will remember most about this person…

Name

Address

City, State, and Zip Code

Phone

E-mail

What I will remember most about this person…

Name

Address

City, State, and Zip Code

Phone

E-mail

What I will remember most about this person…

Name	Name
Address	Address
City, State, and Zip Code	City, State, and Zip Code
Phone	Phone
E-mail	E-mail
What I will remember most about this person…	What I will remember most about this person…

Name	Name
Address	Address
City, State, and Zip Code	City, State, and Zip Code
Phone	Phone
E-mail	E-mail
What I will remember most about this person…	What I will remember most about this person…

Name	Name
Address	Address
City, State, and Zip Code	City, State, and Zip Code
Phone	Phone
E-mail	E-mail
What I will remember most about this person…	What I will remember most about this person…

Name	Name
Address	Address
City, State, and Zip Code	City, State, and Zip Code
Phone	Phone
E-mail	E-mail
What I will remember most about this person…	What I will remember most about this person…

Name

Address

City, State, and Zip Code

Phone

E-mail

What I will remember most about this person...

Name

Address

City, State, and Zip Code

Phone

E-mail

What I will remember most about this person...

Name

Address

City, State, and Zip Code

Phone

E-mail

What I will remember most about this person...

Name

Address

City, State, and Zip Code

Phone

E-mail

What I will remember most about this person...

Name

Address

City, State, and Zip Code

Phone

E-mail

What I will remember most about this person...

Name

Address

City, State, and Zip Code

Phone

E-mail

What I will remember most about this person...

Name

Address

City, State, and Zip Code

Phone

E-mail

What I will remember most about this person...

Name

Address

City, State, and Zip Code

Phone

E-mail

What I will remember most about this person...

Until next year...

If you're reading this page, then you are now well-equipped for your summer camp experience. Good for you! You are ready to embark on a journey of discovery, excitement, and—most of all—*fun*. You're ready to tie-dye, make new friends, rule on the Capture the Flag playing field, sing songs, act in skits, tell great stories, and so much more. Everyone has a different experience at camp, and we wish you the greatest adventure of your life. Try new things, get to know new people, and have the best summer ever!

Or, maybe you've come to the end of this book at the same time you've come to the end of summer camp. We hope our tips have been helpful, and have made your camp experience more special and absolutely awesome! Let this one be the beginning of many great summers in the future.

Good luck and see you next summer!

Happy camping,
Chris and Ron

CREDITS

"Questions to ask Camp Directors" reprinted from www.CampParents.org by permission of the American Camp Association®; copyright 2007 American Camping Association®, Inc.

Original Frisbee® Disc is a registered trademark of Wham-o, Inc.

··

INDEX

ABOUT THE AUTHORS

RON DEFAZIO is a 4th-grade teacher in Waterbury, Connecticut. He is also the Director of YMCA Summer Day Camp Mataucha in Watertown, Connecticut, where he has been a member of the staff for thirteen years.

CHRIS PALLATTO is the Executive Director of the Wheeler Regional Family YMCA in Connecticut, and has served in various camp-management positions for more than fifteen years.

Chris and Ron run the website www.ultimatecampresource.com.

ABOUT THE ILLUSTRATOR

ETHAN LONG loved camping as a child. He still does, but never goes. If he did, he would definitely need this handbook. Seeing that he is 41 years old at the time of this publication, going to summer camp doesn't really apply to him. So he lives comfortably with his wife and three kids in their air-conditioned home in Orlando, Florida.